First Aid

for

Tantrums

by

Kathy Levinson, Ph.D.

SATURN PRESS

II. First Aid for Tantrums
Copyright © 1997 by Kathy Levinson, Ph.D.
First Edition

Library of Congress Catalog Card Number: 96-93066
International Standard Book Number: 1-885843-04-6

Printed in the United States of America

Cover design by Lightbourne Images, Inc.
Interior illustrations by Anne Marie Walsh

Published by:
Saturn Press, Inc.
17639 Foxborough Lane
Boca Raton, FL 33496

Acknowledgments

It's a funny thing how an idea can pop into your head when you least expect it. I was sitting at my desk working on another book when I heard a rumble in the kitchen between the men of my family. "Of course!" I thought, and threw the manuscript I was working on over my shoulder. *First Aid for Tantrums* was born.

As a school psychologist and family therapist, I have talked to many, many parents over the years. Some I helped and some helped me. When I heard a sensible solution to a childhood dilemma from a parent, I'd keep it to share with other parents along my journey. I would like to thank several moms who have impressed me with their sensitivity, common sense and wisdom and whose ideas are interwoven within this book: Betty Edelman, Maureen Harney, Lorri Kellogg, Gwen Sidlo, and Anne Marie Walsh.

For an idea to make the transition from manuscript to book takes the artful expertise of an experienced editor. I would like to thank Erica Orloff for leading me through this process. She is the consummate professional.

I would like to thank my good friends who always knew what I was up to and where I was going: Sharon Conway, Marcy Sirkin, and Laurie Suskind.

And of course, back to the men of my family: Marc and Peter. To Marc, my husband, who shares the same vision and who encourages me daily to keep reaching further to the stars. To Peter, my son, whose presence in my heart is one of the greatest blessings I have ever known.

*For my son, Peter Walsh Levinson,
whose sensitivity, curiosity, and spirit
never cease to amaze me.*

Contents

Introduction

During the process of writing this book, I routinely thought about the message I wanted to see interwoven throughout the text. The message that I want you to take away from the reading of my book. In my experiences as a school psychologist and family therapist, I often found that moms and dads are the most concerned about their children's behavior, especially tantrums. That word alone has the ability to give a parent that deer in the headlights look. Over the years, many parents voiced concerns that perhaps they weren't skilled enough at parenting, or that something was seriously wrong with their children. Why was being a parent so hard sometimes?

Being a parent is the most important responsibility in your lifetime. And the truth is that parenting a child is both difficult and wonderful. There are those precious moments that you wish you could hold onto in your memory forever. Even as I write this passage to you, my little boy is giving me one of those moments. Although he should have been asleep an hour ago, he is calling out to me from his crib. "Mom." "Yes, Peter." "I'm doing okay. I'm comfy." I know that when he is all grown-up, my heart will long to hear those simple words just one more time.

Then there are those other moments when you feel as if you have 20 monkeys on your back and you can't find your patience anywhere. You know that your child is special and wonderful and all that, but at this moment you are burning up your supply of rocket fuel. You know you're going to blow at any minute.

Like little birds learning to spread their wings and leave the nest, our children are learning to open their personalities and become independent from us. The process begins the moment they enter our world. It isn't easy. There are all those emotions and urges to experience and get a handle on. There's language to develop and relationships to understand. And we haven't even gotten to all those social and cultural nuances, or learning right from wrong. High school chemistry has nothing up on this course load.

Tantrums are often a normal part of this process. Tantrums are sometimes the only way for little ones to tell us that they disagree, feel frustrated, feel tired or hungry, or are overwhelmed. For some parents, the word tantrum evokes an image of a screaming child throwing furniture through a living room window. Not at all. In some rare cases, tantrums can be extreme, but for the great majority, tantrums are short-lived episodes of tears and frustration that disappear as a child matures.

This book was written with the desire to help you get through this sometimes challenging stage of your child's development. You'll find that the book is filled with solutions for a variety of life situations ranging from the dinner hour to the supermarket to airplane trips. I have also included a chapter written just for you that discusses lifestyles, stress, and the importance of finding balance in our lives.

Prologue:

My First Tantrum

I survived my first tantrum on board the Fire Island Ferry. I decided to take my one year old with me to do some shopping on Long Island. Anyone who travels with a baby knows that you drag along a lot of "stuff." Between the stroller and the suitcase-sized baby bag in one arm and your squirming child in the other, it's a wonder you can walk, much less travel.

It was a beautiful summer morning, and I wanted to sit outside on the upper deck. But as I stared up the narrow stairs leading to the upper deck and looked down at all this paraphernalia I was lugging, I opted for plan B. I decided to sit down quickly on the nearest available bench.

With one free hand, I opened the stroller and placed my son comfortably into it. Hopeful that the motion of the ferry would put him to sleep, I took out my coffee and began to read the paper. Perfect.

After what seemed like a nanosecond, my son's face changed from a smile to a frown. I calmly offered him a bottle, barely glancing up from my paper. He threw it at me. A cracker . . . smashed to the floor. Keys . . . slam. His body started twisting and struggling as if taken over by baby demons. This was not going to be pretty. I put the coffee and my newspaper away.

3

Thinking fast, I held my son up to the window so he could see the water. This worked for a while . . . all of 20 seconds. Then the shrieking started. Loud shrieking. He was shrieking so loudly I, and all the passengers, could hear him over the roar of the ferry's engines.

It's important to understand that a 20-ton steel ferry bouncing along at 30 knots is not the best place for a baby to walk. Of course, a baby doesn't know that. What my son did know was that this ferry was a cool place to check out and I was definitely in the way. Furious that I would not let him walk, my son let out a scream that started way down in his toes, gathered steam, and, with blood-curdling effect, shot out of his mouth. With the strength of a thousand babies he tried to break free.

Being a genius, I recognized the situation for what it was. My son was having his first tantrum. In the back of my head I heard a squeaky little voice asking, "So, Miss Smarty Psychologist, what are you going to do now?"

I could feel every set of eyes behind me burning through the back of my head like lasers. When I dared to turn around, the faces were ugly; not an empathetic passenger in the bunch. As if they've never been in my position. Really. Their expressions asked me, "What's the matter? Can't you keep that kid quiet? How did he get so spoiled?" I turned around and never looked back again.

With tears and perspiration running down his face, my son was a madman. I locked my arms around him and held on for the ride. By the time the ferry reached the marina, my son was exhausted. Once in the car, he fell asleep instantly.

As for me, I drove away wondering how I handled my first tantrum and what I could have done differently. And I knew that I had better be ready for the next one.

Chapter 1

Diagnosis: Tantrums

A new parent brings home a tiny infant. The mother rhapsodizes a while about the baby's perfect little fingers and toes. The delicious newborn smell of her baby. The father stands over the crib while his little daughter sleeps and marvels at her angelic appearance as he feels his heart swell. Each parent understands that this is a love like no other. They cope with sleepless nights and revel in each of baby's new accomplishments.

The baby grows. Her parents start hearing about this mysterious "monster" called the "terrible two's." Not our baby, they think. Then one day the parents awake to discover their cherubic little baby has somehow been transformed. Gone is the happy, peaceful little tyke of their memory. She has been replaced by a demanding, kicking stubborn little fireplug who always has to have her way. Of all the things that fluster a parent, dealing with and understanding a tantrum may be the biggest dilemma.

What is a Tantrum?

Close your eyes. Imagine for a moment a little child with clenched fists, red face, tears streaming down his face, probably lying on the floor, screaming at full lung capacity. Can you see it? That's a tantrum.

We all have our own pet names for tantrums. Some will say that a child is "losing it" or "throwing a fit" or even "having a meltdown." Any way you describe it, we all seem to know that you're talking about a tantrum. It is a universal language all its own.

What seems to startle most parents is the suddenness with which a tantrum appears. One moment your child is smiling and in the next second he or she is having an uncontrollable explosion of tears, complete with flailing body parts and a lot of screaming.

Take heart, tantrums are a normal part of a child's development, first appearing at about one year or when your child starts to walk and easing up by age six. That is not to say, however, that tantrums miraculously disappear on a child's sixth birthday. Sorry, life is never that predictable. A tantrum or tantrum-like behavior can continue well into adulthood. (You know who you are.) And if you've never seen an adult tantrum, get to a department store the day after Thanksgiving or Christmas.

The Birth of a Tantrum

A tantrum is born the moment those two little baby feet touch the ground. Once your child begins to walk and move around independently, a new chapter begins in his or her life and yours. Now for the first time, with feet in motion, there are places to go, people to see, and lots of potential trouble to get into.

Prior to this new walking stage, life was simpler, safer, and more comfortable — for parents. If the baby cried, you offered her a bottle or a pacifier. If he seemed irritable, you checked his diaper, fed him, or laid him down for a nap. With the exception of a brief crawling stage, babies are more or less carried and put wherever their parents want them to be. Now with feet on the ground, albeit wobbly, your baby is ready to move.

Frustration: The Root of the Problem

Young children have tantrums for a variety of reasons but the basis for it all is frustration. For the first 12 months of a baby's life, babies usually have their own way and very few, if any, restrictions are placed on them. Then, not long after, children start exploring their way through the house, and they start hearing a nagging foreign word, "No."

Filled with curiosity and excitement, little children want to touch and taste things in their world. Young children learn by feeling different textures and using their sensations of taste, sight, and smell. Unfortunately, without an awareness of what could be dangerous or even deadly, little children need to be carefully watched.

As his tiny finger reaches into a wall socket, a little child is likely to hear, "No! You can't touch that. No. No." Or when she finds a cabinet full of house cleaners and aerosol cans to bang on the floor, "No, no. You can't do that. Dangerous." And when little hands go in the dog's mouth when Rex is eating, "No. Get away from the dog when he's eating. Don't do that." "No, no, no, no." Imagine how confusing this word is to understand. Imagine how frustrating.

Uncalibrated Frustration Meters

Just as we are not born with the ability to walk or talk, we are not born with the ability to cope with frustration. Like motor skills or language, it is a skill to be developed and learned.

Consider for a moment the thermostat in your home. The thermostat is calibrated and set to respond to the variations of temperature in your home. When the temperature in the house becomes too warm, the thermostat reacts by shutting the heat off. If the thermostat were not calibrated or sensitive to change there would be no way to control your home's temperature.

Our emotions and the way in which we respond to life's daily events is the result of our own internal thermostats or frustration meters. Our frustration meters help us to react differently to varying circumstances, such as whether we missed a plane or let our coffee get cold on the counter. Maturity, insight, and life experiences have helped us to develop calibrated frustration meters. Some things we ignore, some we let slide, and others we make a scene over.

So what about a one- or two-year old child? The same little child who has just learned to walk and is busy exploring every nook and cranny. Forget calibration, this child doesn't even own a frustration meter! The result is the child reacts to any frustrating situation, no matter how bland or how serious, in the same way. He or she explodes into a tantrum.

That is why your child bursts into tears if you give him the wrong cup or throws herself on the ground if you leave a room too fast. The situations are potentially endless until a young child learns to be sensitive to his or her internal frustration meter. From the outside your child could look bratty, but relax, it's very normal. Find your patience and keep your sense of humor and I promise you, you will get through this stage.

Learning to cope and monitor frustration is an ongoing lesson for a child. It is also an ongoing lesson in our adult lives. This must be an enormous task for a toddler who has everything yet to learn.

The importance of learning to manage frustration cannot be understated and is essential in the development of healthy emotional growth. The child who fails to learn this lesson can become self-serving, demanding, and insensitive to the feelings of others.

Those who successfully learn to handle frustration are at an advantage as adults. They are the ones who know to listen before speaking, are tolerant of the flaws in others, can persevere in adversity, and are willing to take on the tough tasks. Think of a well-respected, accomplished individual and you are likely to find a well-calibrated frustration meter.

Frustration and Beyond

With frustration the likely catalyst for most tantrums, there are other factors that can upset this delicate balance. Understanding and identifying tantrum triggers helps you to help your child.

Finding the Right Words

Most children between the ages of one and three years do not yet have the language skills to satisfactorily express their feelings, desires, and needs. Although they may be able to say 100+ different words and even string two- to three-word sentences together, children this age lack the language development to fully express themselves. As a result, when a child gets overly frustrated and communication is limited, the tantrum is most likely to appear.

It's not out of the oridinary for a little one at this stage to exasperate mom or dad. With all the screaming going on, a parent knows that his or her child wants something, but what? Sometimes the situation calls for a process of elimination. For example, you have figured out that your child is hungry. The next thing to determine is what would your child like to eat? A cookie? More juice? Don't be surprised if the thing your child decides upon is the very first thing you offered him.

Independence vs. Dependence

Little children between the ages of one and three are sometimes caught in a double-bind. They love the independence of being able to walk and move about freely but still depend on their parents for approval and support. That's why a simple decision such as "Should I or should I not go up these stairs?" can bring on a sudden tantrum. The child wants to go up the stairs because it is a new adventure but at the same time needs mom or dad to tell her that she can.

Sometimes Kids Run Out of Gas

Being too tired can cause a tantrum in just about anyone, regardless of their age. But this occurs most commonly in children between the ages of one and five. Sometimes enthusiasm for what they are doing prevents them from slowing down or taking a rest even when that would be best. Children of this age usually don't recognize when their gas tanks are near empty and will run and run until they literally can't anymore. Exhaustion or a tantrum (or both) soon follow.

And Sometimes They're Just Bored

Although little children seem fascinated with even the most mundane things, they can also experience boredom. Young toddlers between ages one and three don't always know how to keep themselves entertained. In other situations, such as waiting rooms or inside places of worship, children can have a difficult time sitting patiently. There simply isn't enough going on to keep them interested. (See page 11 for Boredom Busters)

Hunger Monsters

Hunger is most likely to cause a tantrum in young children who do not yet have the language skills to effectively express what they want. Tantrums typically erupt when their requests go unnoticed and your child becomes frustrated. That's why it is a wise idea to keep good snacks close by.

A Boredom Buster: Activity Box

Use a shoe box, old stationery box, briefcase, fishing box, or even a baby wipes container to hold a few interesting things your child would enjoy playing with. Decorate the outside with stickers and individualize it to your child.

Ideas for fun things inside:

+ crayons, a coloring book, a pad of paper
+ little windup toys
+ small books
+ stickers
+ a calculator, stop watch, egg timer
+ sunglasses
+ small hand-puppets
+ funny photographs

When Parenting Feels Tough

Being a good parent is the most difficult of jobs. Forget about sports heroes and movie stars. Passing your know-how on to your children so that they can do better is a skill that takes years of dedication, patience, and strength. I've seen plenty of

What is a Good Snack?

+ Foods that are low in fat, salt, or sugar

+ Foods that your children can handle without much help or fuss from you.

+ **Healthy snacks 12 to 18 months:** bananas, fruit muffin, peach puree with cottage cheese, flaked tuna and apple pieces, cheese bits, salt-free pretzels, rice cakes, bagels, soft dried fruit, raisins, chopped grapes, bite-size veggies, fruit slices, yogurt, apple sauce, Cheerios or other unsugared cereals.

> ## What is a Good Snack? *(continued)*
>
> + **Healthy snacks 18 to 24 months:** peanut butter squares on whole grain bread, muffins, yogurt mixed with fresh fruit, cheese and crackers, cold pasta.
>
> + **Healthy snacks 24 to 36 months:** whole wheat pretzels, low-salt crackers, granola squares, ginger cookies, frozen banana slices, frozen mousse, bread sticks.
>
> + **Healthy snacks after age three:** fruit rolls, plain popcorn, peanut butter on unpeeled apple slices, raw vegetable strips.

parents ask themselves, "Where have I messed up? How can I do better?" Unfortunately, there is no set of instructions that comes with parenthood and even the most exemplary moms and dads are self-critical. Knowing where some of the potential land mines are can make the process less difficult for you and your children. Recognizing these land mines can be all the clues you need to divert your child's attention away from a tantrum.

Inconsistency

Children are observant, curious little creatures. It doesn't take them very long to figure out the holes in your parenting style. Are you the parent who means what you say or do you get mushy and weak-kneed? Is what you say open for

> ## What Do Kids Need From Their Parents?
>
> + They need their parents to be consistent when giving correction.
>
> + They need their parents to "mean what they say and say what they mean."
>
> + They need their parents to be fair with discipline.
>
> + They need their parents to avoid power plays and the urge to always be right.

negotiations? Does your "no" mean no or maybe? Do you say to your son that he can't have that candy bar and then give it to him when he starts to cry? Eventually, your children will outsmart you because they learn that if they bug you long enough, you will fold like a deck of cards.

Unstable Marriages

With one in two marriages ending in divorce, many children have to cope with their parents' relationship problems. Although young toddlers cannot understand what may be happening, they do pick up on stress, anger, anxiety, even depression in their parents. Toddlers caught in their parents' divorce can react in a variety of ways. Some may march through the experience unscathed while others may temporarily become demanding because of inconsistent attention, or they can be clingy for fear of abandonment.

Children caught in the throes of their parents' marital problems can demonstrate a broad range of problems such as having trouble at school, getting into fights with other children, lying, stealing, not eating, hyperactivity, and physical complaints. If you are experiencing marital problems and your child is demonstrating behavioral changes, chances are that the marital issues are the catalyst for your child's behavior problems.

Personal Challenges

Nobody ever said being a grown-up is an easy task. Sometimes personal concerns arise that make being an adult and a parent a monumental task. How often have you wished to be a kid again? Issues such as job lay-offs, illness, finances, or drug and alcohol abuse directly influence the behaviors of the children in your household.

Remember homes are like mini-ecological systems. When a life problem surfaces, such as a job lay-off, everyone in the family is affected in some small way. The larger the problem, the more affected family members become.

Too Many Chiefs

With single-parent families or both parents in the work force, children are spending more time in day care centers and after-school programs. Children are corrected and disciplined one way by their caregivers and another when at home with mom and dad. This can be confusing and at times stressful for everyone involved.

A little one in a preschool program may be permitted to do many things that would be forbidden at home. For example, maybe the children are allowed to bounce balls inside because everything is plastic and childproof. When those children come home and try to do the same thing, they may find themselves sternly reprimanded because there are many things in the home that could be broken. These messages can be confusing to a young child who can not yet discriminate the subtle differences between inside at preschool and inside at home.

Additionally, parents must present a united front to their children. Talk about how you are going to handle a particular situation out of earshot from your children because they will be listening. When you disagree or criticize each other's parenting decisions in front of your children, you leave a big, opportunistic hole for children to divide you both. Ever hear, "But Daddy said I could go!"?

Sometimes It's Anyone's Guess

Sometimes children melt down into a tantrum . . . well, just because. I can recall a day just like this with my own son. One minute he was laughing and giggling on the couch next to me, and in the next second he was sobbing. To this day, I don't have a clue what brought this on. But while in the midst of this mystery crying episode, I held him close and rubbed his back until all was well again.

Who Has Tantrums? And More Importantly, When Do They Go Away?

Although some children will never have a tantrum, most will at some point in their development. Tantrums usually appear about the same time your child starts walking, usually around the first birthday. When they go away is entirely up to the individual.

Young children do not hold the patent on a tantrum. On the contrary, tantrums can continue through the teens and into adulthood. Don't panic. With the exception of an occasional tantrum, most children outgrow this tantrum stage by their sixth birthday.

A Few Tantrum Statistics to Rattle Your Nerves

+ **One year olds:**
  14% have tantrums every day

+ **Two and three year olds:**
  20% have two or more tantrums a day

+ **Four year olds:**
  11% have tantrums every day

+ **Five to seventeen year olds:**
  5% demonstrate emotional explosions that look an awful lot like a tantrum.

+ Adults can throw a tantrum, but we usually say they're making a scene . . .

. . . Making a Scene

Pick up any child development book and you will find that tantrums are described as phenomena known only to the young child. I'm not so sure. I've witnessed plenty of tantrums over the years but children weren't throwing them. "Grown-ups" were. These "adults" stamped their feet or screamed to get their own way — kind of looked like a tantrum to me. Of course, when we become adults we don't say that someone is having a tantrum. Instead we say that they are making a scene.

Before becoming a psychologist, I worked my way through graduate school as a waitress in a popular steak house on Long Island's north shore. It was a good restaurant, too. Very upscale. And making a scene was commonplace. Everybody did it. The owners made scenes because the staff was always doing something wrong. On weekends everybody made a scene in front of the hostess' podium because their table wasn't ready. Sophisticated, well-heeled people stamped their Gucci-clad feet, raised their voices and, sometimes, slammed their fists down onto the sacred reservations book.

One busy Saturday night, a well-known comedian, who dined at the steak house often, walked in with a group of friends and no reservation. As the customers parted like the Red Sea for Moses, Mr. Not-So-Funny stepped up to the podium to make a scene.

"I want a table up front. I'm not going to sit way back there. Everybody knows that anybody who sits in the back is a nobody!"

The seasoned owner kept her composure and tried explaining that on such a busy night without a reservation there would be a little wait. She would do the very best she could.

"Unacceptable!" he shouted. "You know who I am. You should give me a table. I shouldn't have to wait . . . ever!"

"I know who you are and I'm delighted that you're here, but we are so busy tonight. Please try to understand, I'll have you seated as soon as I can."

Reluctantly the comedian marched to the available table at the back of the restaurant with his embarrassed friends in tow. Once at the table, he slammed down his drink and scowled. He even barked at the waitress.

> ### . . . Making a Scene *(continued)*
>
> "Will you knock it off, you're acting like a child for God's sake," said a friend.
>
> "There's no excuse. She should have done the right thing. She knows who I am."
>
> "Look, stop it already. This is a nice table."
>
> "It's great," he scowled.
>
> When it was time to take the order, the waitress, keeping a close eye on this so-called funny man, reluctantly returned to his table. He looked up at her and said, "I'm sorry, honey. We're ready to order. Give me zucchini as my side dish."
>
> "We're out of zucchini for the moment. How about apple sauce?"
>
> "Apple sauce? *Apple sauce!*" he shouted incredulously as if just asked to eat a bicycle tire. "You're asking me if I want apple sauce!" roared the comedian. "You show me one person in here who's eating apple sauce. I don't believe this," and then he threw his hands up in the air.
>
> The waitress left the comedian who was now being scolded by his wife and friends. When the waitress returned a few minutes later with their salads, the comedian, barely holding it together, and forcing a smile through clenched teeth said, "Sweetheart, I'm sorry. I'll have apple sauce."
>
> The waitress, knowing the trouble she'd catch from the owner, looked this comedic legend in the eye and said ever-so-sweetly, "I have apple sauce. But I don't have any apple sauce . . . *for you!*" and walked away.

Boys vs. Girls

Though most people will deny it, the battle of the sexes carries into the world of tantrums. I am often asked who is more prone to tantrums, girls or boys? Men seem more inclined to believe that little girls quickly melt away into a sobbing tantrum, while women make a connection between boys, aggression, and tantrums. Although boys are usually cited in the research literature

as being more inclined towards behavioral and learning disabilities in school, they are off the hook this time. Tantrums occur about as often in boys as they do in girls.

Top Tantrum Triggers

While a tantrum can rear its ugly head in any place imaginable, there are certain places where a tantrum is more likely to appear. The following are some common tantrum triggers:

Shopping

Who hasn't seen a child lose it in the supermarket or department store? From ten aisles over you can hear the ever-familiar, "But mommy I want it!" In fact, if we asked our own parents they might say that more than a few of us threw tantrums in a store.

Trains, Planes, and Automobiles

Before having children, my husband always joked about sitting next to the "screaming baby" when traveling. I warned him. I said one day you are going to be the one with the screaming baby. Let's just leave it at that. Trains, planes, and automobiles are often too hot or too cold, and too confining for a child.

Places of Worship

Small children have a real hard time understanding why you can't talk during a service of any kind. It's a difficult idea to grasp; I can talk in a store, a plane, and a library, but I can't talk here. Active and full of energy, little ones have difficulty sitting silently for any length of time.

Waiting Rooms

A waiting room poses two problems for a child. First, he or she is expected to sit quietly until the nurse or receptionist appears. Secondly, children see waiting rooms as spooky, funny-smelling places and wonder, "What are they going to do to me when I get in *there*?"

Restaurants

Most children love to go out to eat with their moms and dads. It's a special treat. But what sometimes happens is that you wait too long to be seated and even longer to be served. Kids lose interest, get hungry, and grow tired of sitting at the table.

Bedtime

While many little ones enjoy the ritual of getting ready for bed others are not yet ready to say good-bye to the day. Some children can create very colorful protests such as, "Can I just ask you a question? I think I have a stomach ache. I'm thirsty. I don't like these pajamas. Can't I sleep with you? Can't I sleep with the dog?"

The Transition Hour

The transition hour is a term for those times when an activity shifts to something else. Dinner time is an example of a transition hour. Your little one has been playing for a while and when you begin to prepare dinner, they ask for your undying attention. You may also see a transition-hour tantrum when daddy comes home from work. While your child is delighted that daddy is home, the transition of mommy and me to mommy, daddy, and me can ruffle his or her feathers.

Rushing Around When You Are Late

How many parents have seen their little ones burst into tantrums just when they are rushing to get out the front door? The problem is really two-fold: you're growing inpatient because of time constraints and your child cannot keep up and soon becomes frustrated. Additionally, the notion of having to rush can be confusing. "Why are we moving so fast? Why are you getting so mad at me?"

The "No" Word

As much as we all dislike it, children and that "no" word just do not mix. The two can be like oil and water. If you don't believe me, try throwing it around with your child for a day. "No" becomes like a little trigger that causes your son or daughter to do things you never expected. You're in the doctor's office and you say, "No Nicky, we don't touch those buttons." The next thing you know little Nicky has that devilish gleam in his eye and his hand is reaching for that big, clunky plug in the electric socket.

The Bright Side of Tantrums

+ Children outgrow them.
+ Tantrums are a normal part of a child's development.
+ Tantrums teach children about tolerating frustration.

 + Tantrums teach children how to cope and problem solve.

Chapter 2

Senzible Solutionz

Although some parents are curious as to why tantrums happen in the first place, all parents want to know how to make them stop! Tantrums stir up feelings in a parent that are uncomfortable to say the very least. Have you ever been near a fire alarm when it suddenly and accidentally goes off? In the midst of that piercing noise, have you ever noticed anybody casually wondering what set it off? It's doubtful. Instead, people scramble, trying to figure out how to turn the darn thing off, panicking, shouting, growing nervous. Tantrums are sort of like fire alarms; they startle you about six inches off the ground when they go off and your immediate goal is to get that child quiet.

Just Tell Me What To Do

When it comes to discipline, parents can get a little uneasy. Your child does something wrong and you have to step in as the "heavy." Sometimes your solution works and sometimes it fails miserably. You look around at other parents and notice that some have no control while others seem to glide right through. What's the difference? Why does it seem as if my child is having more tantrums than other children?

How Do Tantrums Make Parents Feel?

- Nervous
- Anxious
- Inadequate
- Frustrated
- Embarrassed
- Guilty
- More Guilty

Being a good disciplinarian doesn't mean that you know how to be tough or intimidating. It doesn't even mean that you know what to do all the time. Honestly, who does? But being a good disciplinarian does means that you know how to be fair and consistent when correcting your child. You understand the underlying importance of discipline because it is not the punishment that matters so much as what is learned from the lesson. Intervening with your child's tantrum is your way of teaching him or her how to cope with disappointment and frustration.

Learning Right From Wrong

When your children are young, you instill the understanding of right from wrong. This lesson continues throughout your children's development but the foundation is started early. For children to learn from your correction, they need to understand the reason for it. That's important because you will not always be around to make sure that they are doing the right thing or coping with a frustrating situation. For example, it would be better for your children to understand that running out into the street after a toy can be dangerous because they could be hit by a car rather than because they could get in trouble from you.

I have some special memories of my dad who died well before his time when I was just ten years old. Every Saturday,

I tagged along with my dad on his errands. We would head for the deli, the soda distributor, the bakery, and finish up at my favorite stop, the candy store. I can't say for sure how old I was, but I know that I was under four when my father taught me a lesson that is still vivid in my mind today. While my dad was talking to the candy store owner, I reached up and selected a roll of Life Savers from the candy shelf.

It was innocent enough; I saw something I wanted so I took it. When we were pulling away from the curb my father looked down at the roll of Life Savers in my hand and stopped the car. "Where did you get that?" he asked. "From the store, Daddy" I answered innocently. "Don't you know that you can't just take something and not pay for it? That's stealing. Come on, we have to go back inside and pay the man for the candy." Up until that moment in my life I never understood that when you want something in a store, you must buy it. Let's call it my big "A-ha." My dad parked the car and walked me inside the candy store where we paid the owner for my Life Savers. What I remember clearly is how important it was for my dad that I understand that not paying for things in a store is stealing. I also remember that my dad didn't embarrass me or make me feel stupid. He just wanted me to understand that what I did was wrong. I learned my lesson and it never happened again.

Respecting the Rights and Feelings of Other People

Toddlers are naturally self-centered little people, but with careful guidance they can grow into caring, empathetic adults.

Respecting the rights and feelings of others is a learning process. In a toddler's world of "One for me, none for you," he or she needs your help early in this learning process. You can start early by asking your toddler to share a cookie with you. First he or she takes a bite then you take one. When your son or daughter offers you the cookie praise him or her for being kind and willing to share. After all, it is your approval that your child wants most of all.

Developing Self-Control and Frustration Tolerance

You understand that your child needs to learn that the real world is not like Burger King and you can't always have it your way.

Our job as mom or dad is to do the very best we can for our children, but that doesn't mean that we are to attend to their every whim and desire. Doing so ultimately creates an unpopular little person frequently referred to as a spoiled brat. When your child wants something, like a cookie instead of dinner, simply explain that this is not an option. If he or she pouts or starts to cry, hold your ground, "We don't eat cookies for dinner." Most children love to be helpers when it comes to grown-up things. You might suggest, "Why don't you give me a hand and help set the table or wash the lettuce for the salad." Smaller children may need simple redirection to another activity such as a puzzle or coloring book.

Growing Up to be Happy and Healthy

An undisciplined child is often disliked by his peers because of his tendency to be self-centered and impulsive. As a parent you understand that the road to adulthood is built on lessons, both big and small. When you discipline your child you help him or her to internalize those lessons for the monumental challenges later on.

Some Thoughts to Live By

Over the years I've met many parents who struggle with the issue of how to be a good parent. They struggle with what is read in magazines, presented on news programs, in contrast to how they were raised, and what they feel in their hearts. With our world moving at a seemingly faster and faster pace, it is easy to lose sight of the right path.

In this section, I've compiled a list of suggestions that seem to stand the test of time. I think of them as little pearls of wisdom that I have accumulated over the years from working with parents. Some or all of these suggestions would eventually come up when speaking with parents. Keep them close to your heart and mind and you will be successful with your children:

Know Your Own Child

No two children are the same, even if they live under the same roof. There aren't universal rules for discipline that apply to all children in the same way. Be sensitive and alert to your child's temperament and the ways in which he or she learns best. Some children need a time-out chair while others only need a firm stare.

Match Your Discipline With Your Child's Developmental Level

Understanding where your child is developmentally is important if you would like to be effective with your interventions. Every stage carries behaviors that parents would like to eliminate but which are completely normal. Children, as they grow and learn, try out all sorts of behaviors, including aggression. They learn from the consequences created and from their parents' reactions. A child may try something several times just to see what happens to mom and dad. It's not out of spite but out of curiosity and a insatiable desire to learn.

3 to 5 Months

A young baby who is breast-feeding may bite down on his or her mom's nipple. This can be quite uncomfortable if the baby has started to get teeth. The mom should take the baby away from the nipple briefly and then continue breast-feeding a moment or two later. The baby is simply trying out those new teeth and is not actually trying to hurt his or her mother. If your child needs to teethe use a pacifier.

7 to 12 Months

As babies develop, they become more alert and curious about the people and things around them. A sparkling earring may be fun to pull or an eye may be interesting to poke. Children at this age like to grab whatever is in their reach . . . your hair, sunglasses, or jewelry. They will scratch and pinch, stick their fingers in your mouth or eyes, all because they are curious. A child in his or her parent's arms is in close proximity to a very exciting place, your face. When your child pulls your earring or sticks his or her finger in your eye, you react. Your reaction is fun because your child is starting to explore cause-and-effect relationships. You might gently take your child's hand and say, "Be nice with mommy. Touch nicely like this," while slowly moving baby's hand over your face. If your child is pulling your hair say, "When you pull my hair that hurts mommy. Don't pull my hair. Touch softly like this" and demonstrate with baby's hand on his or her own head. If your child will not stop, then put him or her down, explaining your actions, wait a moment and then pick your child up again.

12 to 15 Months

One day when you are playing or cuddling with your child, you may be startled by a sharp, stinging pain on your arm, thigh, or breast. You may even see stars. Your child is up to it again; doing that learning and exploring thing. A child will bite down on your stomach to experience the sensation of biting and your reaction to it. Be careful not to overreact or frighten your little one as a hard bite on a tender part of the body can evoke quite a reaction. Instead, stop the activity, explain that the bite hurt, and that he or she is not to do it again. After a few moments hug your child and say, "We hug each other. No biting. Biting hurts. Hugs are better."

16 to 30 Months

This is often the time when a child challenges the word "No." You may tell your little one not to step off the curb and she'll look right at you with a devilish grin and step down onto the street. Your child is testing you and asking herself, "Does Dad really mean what he says?" Children commonly act surprised that they have gotten into trouble because to children it is a game. Make your correction swift and clear: "I told you not to step into the street. It is dangerous."

Also at this time your child may start biting, hitting, or scratching other children. You're usually at a playground, the children are excited, and in the next second someone gets a scratch. We all have a tendency to overreact when this happens, but don't panic. Tend to the child who may have been hurt, but don't overlook the child who delivered the bite or scratch. You may notice that he or she is the most surprised that the other child is hurt and by your reaction. Intervene quickly and clearly, explaining that it is not okay to strike other children. Explain what will happen if this behavior continues, such as your child being removed from the play area or losing the toy, etc.

Although tantrums can appear as early as 9 or 10 months, they typically make their debut at this time. The tantrums seem to come out of nowhere and are sometimes unavoidable. There's a lot going on in your child's head right about now . . . a true struggle between independence and dependence. Make sure your child is in a safe place, step back, and let the tantrum run its course. When the tantrum is over, go to your child and offer a hug and some soothing talk. Remember, the more you try to undo the tantrum the worse it will become. In other words, the more involved you become with your child's tantrum, the more intense it will become, and the longer it will last. Tantrums have a tendency to feed on attention, no matter what flavor or variety. There are two key times to intervene with a tantrum: either before it occurs or after it is over. As your child becomes older and can be reasoned with, discuss that you understand how hard it is to be two and a half or three years old . . . but only after the tantrum is over.

3 to 6 Years

Your child is no longer a baby but a miniature person. Children at this age express feelings, have definite opinions and experience worry or anxiety when realizing they are in trouble. Outbursts may take a dramatic turn, such as storming off, slamming bedroom doors, or smashing things in a rage. You may find yourself wondering what it will be like when he or she is a teenager! Decide for yourself whether or not you can ignore the drama of a slammed door or your child storming out of the room. You can't, however, ignore your child when he or she smashes things in a fit of anger. Intervene quickly, letting your child know that throwing or smashing things is unacceptable because it is both dangerous and out of control. If your child is very upset, hold him or her firmly until the rage passes. When the worst is over, talk about what happened, why throwing things is a bad idea, and how he or she might be feeling. Then discuss acceptable alternatives to get anger or frustration across.

6 Years and Beyond

Tantrums at this age can take on the look of an adult squabble because your child's protests are usually verbal. There may be great protests that you are an unfair or bad parent, as well as impassioned pleas for "fairness." Some children are quite adept at making their parents feel guilty or just plain

Quick Tantrum Tamers

Age	What the Tantrum Could Look Like	What You Can Do
0–8 months	Infants don't have tantrums. Always go to your baby when he or she seems uncomfortable. Crying or fussing is their way of communicating their needs to you, whether it be a bottle, diaper change, nap, change of position, or they don't feel well.	
9–18 months	A sudden explosion of tears and crying. Children may throw themselves to the ground, stiffen their bodies, and clench their fists.	You have a few choices: Redirect or distract your child to another activity; pick your child up and gently soothe him or her; sit with your child in a quiet place until calm.
18 months– 3 years	Screaming and crying, protesting, slamming toys or cabinet doors, throwing objects to the ground, lying on the ground while flailing arms and legs.	Redirection to another activity can still be effective at this age. Depending on the seriousness of the tantrum, you can choose to ignore it or you might carry your child to a safe quiet place, remind your child that he or she is out of line, and stay close by until calm.
3–6 years	Screaming and crying, protesting, making demands, physical resistance, throwing objects, maybe some biting or hitting.	Give a clear and simple warning that this behavior is inappropriate and remind child of the consequences. If your child doesn't listen then remove him or her to another quiet room and say, "When you have calmed down, you may come back out and join us."
6 years and beyond	Loud verbal protests, defiance, dramatic displays of slamming doors, throwing objects, outright refusal, shouting insults, cursing.	Give a clear message that your child is misbehaving, remind him or her of your house rules, "There is no cursing in our home" and make clear your consequences. You might insist that your child leave the room, go to his or her bedroom for a specific time, or take away a privilege.

rotten. Don't be surprised by a slammed bedroom door or shouts of "I can't stand you. I wish you weren't even my mother!" There are several ways to intervene in these explosions. First, learn to recognize the types of situations that may set your child off. Some children don't like to stop doing something they really enjoy, whether it be playing outside, watching TV, or sitting in front of the computer. You might consider giving your child a warning such as, "You're coming inside in ten minutes" or "At the end of this TV show it's time for bed." Now many kids will try to finagle more time by using stalling techniques like "I said I'm coming!" or pretending not to hear you at all. Hold your ground, keep your patience, and stick to your plan. If the situation continues, stay calm, and issue a consequence.

Consequences are a valuable piece in teaching children good behaviors because they enable them to make the connection between actions and results. Frequently the only way to learn the connection between one's actions and the consequences is to experience it firsthand.

Get in Touch With Your Own Instincts

As important as it is for you to know your own child, it is equally important for you to be in touch with your own instincts or gut feelings. Each one of us has this ability, it's just that some are more "in tune" than others. Getting in touch with your instincts will help you to know how to respond to your child. Is what your child did something you can ignore or does it call for stronger measures? And is this a good time to teach a lesson?

Develop your instincts to know when it would be a good time to intervene with your child and when it would not. Often parents fail to use their instincts or gut feelings about a situation and wind up losing the battle and feeling very frustrated. For example, teaching good behavior at the dinner table begins at home and not when you are a dinner guest at someone's home. If your little one is permitted to climb in and out of the booster seat or throw food on the floor at home, then you cannot expect better behavior someplace else. Reinforcing good table manners every day enables your child to understand that we behave this way at "all" dinner tables. Children as young as 15 months have the ability to learn how to properly behave at a table. Give your child a napkin and show him or her how to use it by demonstrating on yourself. "Are you all done eating? Where's your napkin? Let's wipe your fingers off. Don't forget your mouth. You are such a big girl now." Do this every day and your child will start picking up the napkin without being reminded. By the way, your friends will be amazed.

No Child Behaves All the Time

All children, no matter how terrific, will misbehave from time to time. Children learn from experimenting, curiosity, and trying cause-and-effect on everything in their world. Parents included. That's why your toddler may bang his spoon on his plate while keeping one eye on you. He's experimenting with your relationship. "At what point will Mommy tell me to stop?" Toddlers typically move through brief stages where they are delightful one moment and ill-tempered the next. Children need to spread their personality "wings" from time to time, and when it happens keep in mind that there's learning going on.

> When kids start to come apart and unravel . . . they need their parents to be in control.

Let the Punishment Fit the Crime

A child who is punished harshly for having done something wrong does not learn his or her lesson any better. While in every household we have different views about what is an important privilege, carefully consider the fairness of your intervention before taking action.

Example:
Your bath mat is sopping wet. The walls are speckled with water drops. Your child has had a field day in the bathroom. Water, water everywhere.

Punishment that does not fit:
You take away television privileges for a week.

Punishment that fits:
You encourage responsibility by insisting he or she help in the clean up.

Be Consistent

Remember the adage "Say what you mean and mean what you say"? Well it *really* applies when it comes to parenting. If you want to be taken seriously by your children and have any credibility then you must be consistent. If jumping on the bed is forbidden today but permitted tomorrow, the only message sent is that rules have no meaning. If you want to make an exception in certain situations, then explain your reasons for it.

Follow Through

You're only shooting blanks if you don't follow through on your discipline. Your child will figure this one out in about a split second and do what comes logically, tune you out. Warning "You'll go to your room if you do that again" and doing nothing when the "again" occurs is ineffective parenting.

Example:
Your child is tormenting the dog by deliberately hitting poor Junior with a ball.

Ineffective parenting:
"I told you not to hit the dog with the ball. How many times do I have to warn you?" then a few seconds later . . . "Don't make me tell you again!"

Effective parenting:
"I told you that if you hit the dog again with the ball you would go to your room. I want you in your room for the next 15 minutes. Let's go now."

Catch Your Child Being Good

You can become quite effective as a disciplinarian if you look for opportunities to praise and reward your children. Children, after all, want their parents' love and attention. Getting a warm hug from mom or dad just for watching television quietly is a lot more fun than going to time-out for being noisy.

How to zay I Love You

+ Hide a funny or special photograph inside your child's lunch box or between the pages of a favorite book.

+ Cut out a funny cartoon from a newspaper or magazine and slip it under your child's door or place it in a book bag.

+ Write a special note, draw a simple heart or kiss, and place it somewhere your child will find it.

+ Make up a coupon (handwritten is fine) telling your child that he or she is entitled to an ice cream after school, a rental movie on Friday night, or a visit to a special place. Why? Just because.

+ Pick out a special ring, medallion, necklace, or watch that you both can wear. Not necessarily something expensive, but something that bonds the two of you together.

How to Say I Love You *(continued)*

+ Share a secret wink or nod that only you two know about.
+ Put a special day on the calendar, monthly if you can, that belongs only to you and your child. Plan the day together.
+ Reserve some quiet, personal time in your day to talk with each other face to face.
+ At bedtime, tell the "story" of your child's birth or adoption.
+ Keep an album or scrapbook of keepsakes and photographs and look through them together from time to time.
+ Don't be afraid to stop being an adult for just a little while and play with your child.
+ Simply say, "I love you."

Learning About Consequences

This is one of the more important life lessons that not everybody learns but should. If you keep putting your French fries in the soda, then it will get "icky" and you will have none to drink. Put your book in the toilet and it will get ruined. Unless the act was accidental, allow your child to experience the natural consequences of his or her behaviors.

Give an Explanation For Your Discipline

Explain to your child why he or she is being punished without going into a long-winded dialogue or a heated debate. Even toddlers can understand to a certain degree that you are taking away the remote control because they keep throwing it on the floor.

Find and Keep Your Patience

Above all else, keep hold of your patience. If you feel your patience being tried and fear you may lose it, take a break from your child until you feel it returning. All children can be tenacious when it comes to getting their own way. Remember that toddlers have a fleeting attention span and short memories. They can be distracted easily and often need gentle reminders. Older children need to be reminded in a simple, clear manner that their behavior could get them in trouble.

Perhaps the boxed guidelines on patience will help you find and keep your patience:

Learning to keep your Patience

Short-Term:

1. Take a deep breath and wait about 5 to 10 seconds before speaking.
2. Leave the room or area for a few moments and then return to the scene.

Long-Term:

1. Learn to recognize and separate the situations that are no big deal and the ones that need your immediate reaction. Try to keep things in perspective.
2. Recognize when *you* are overtired or overstressed and take some time out for yourself. For example, take a walk or a hot bath.
3. You can't always be supermom or superdad . . . ask for help when you need it.
4. Find and practice your own regimen of relaxation techniques.
5. Although this can be difficult, always try to look for the humor in the situation.

Ask Your Child For His or Her Opinion

Before an incident happens or while your child is behaving ask him or her what, in your child's own opinion, an appropriate intervention would be. For example, "What should happen if you don't come home for dinner when I call you?" Remember it and use it when the situation arises. If it works,

give your child credit and remind your child that it was his or
her idea.

If It Doesn't Work, Stop Using It

If you find that a particular intervention fails consistently,
then it is senseless to keep using it. For example, as popular as
it is, not all children benefit from time-out. How do you know
if your solution to your child's tantrums is failing and should
be tossed out? Consider for a moment the following questions
and you might find your answer:

✚ Is my child's behavior getting better or worse?
✚ Does my child consider this to be a true consequence?
✚ Have I used this intervention so many times that my
   child thinks I sound like a broken record?
✚ Am I all talk and no action? How often do I really
   follow through?
✚ Am I giving my child a consequence that I can truly stay
   on top of, such as no telephone privileges for six months?
✚ Have I piled so many consequences on top of my
   child that he or she feels the situation is hopeless. In
   other words, "Why bother to change? I'm punished
   for life anyway."

The Art of Using
Time-Out

The idea of using time-out with your child can conjure up
images of padded rooms or kids strapped into chairs. It doesn't
have to be that way at all. The term time-out may have originated
from behavioral psychology but parents have been using it
long before they knew what it was called. Weren't you ever

sent to your room as a child? Didn't your dad ever make you sit out a game because you were too wild?

In this section I want to go through some of the fine points of time-out and the reasons why many parents are unsuccessful when using it. Whatever solutions you may choose for your child's misbehaving remember the following important points:

✚ Know your child and what interventions best suit his or her personality.
✚ Be clear and straightforward in your explanations.
✚ Follow your gut feelings when deciding what can and cannot be ignored.
✚ Find your patience and hold onto it with all your might. A sense of humor doesn't hurt either.
✚ Once the situation is over, move on and forget about it.

The Basic Idea Behind Time-Out

This type of intervention can be used to help an out-of-control toddler calm down and regain good behavior or to give an older child the opportunity to think about what he or she has done wrong. It also teaches both age groups that their behavior

How Long Should a Child Be In Time-Out?

General rule: 1 minute for every year of the child.

Example: 5 years old = 5 minutes in time-out

Toddler, 2 and under: 10 to 30 seconds can be enough.

The Exception: Some children need more time to calm down no matter what their age. Some toddlers may need 15 minutes to regain their composure while some 7 year olds require 30 minutes.

was not okay and that you as parent are there to teach them about good behavior.

Where Should a Child Be Timed-Out?

A child needs to be timed-out in a safe place where you can see him or her.

If your child is under age two, you might lay him or her gently on a carpeted area in your house . . . either in your child's own room or some other quiet place. A crib may not be appropriate because children in the midst of a tantrum might throw themselves down and hit the side of a crib.

For a toddler under age two, 15 seconds could be a long time. Don't fall into a power struggle and force your little one to stay put — that's not the reason for using time-out. You might say, "I can see that you're very upset. I'm going to lay you down here until you are feeling better. I'll be right here when you're better." When the crying subsides, you can say "Hey kiddo, there you are. It's good to see you. I want to give you a hug."

Is this coddling? No, because little children under age two don't get upset for the same reasons as older children, nor do they understand the situation in the same way. Children at this tender age can have a tantrum just because they can't decide which doorway to walk through — putting them in a room alone with a door shut only compounds the situation.

If your child is over age three, a special chair can be used as a time-out chair. The chair should be in a safe place away from anything that could harm your child. The toddler should be walked to the chair and not be permitted to talk with anyone while sitting there. A kitchen egg timer works well to let children know that they cannot leave time-out until they hear the timer sound.

Using Time-Out Correctly and Safely

As a therapist, I've heard horror stories of time-out used to extremes. When used correctly and with safety and love as prime considerations, this can be a very effective disciplinary measure. Let common sense and a few basic rules guide you.

Time-Out Should be in a Safe and Nonfrightening Place

Fear has no place in the healthy development of a child. A terrified child doesn't learn how to improve his or her behavior through fear. Instead, the terrified child learns to fear the parent who is creating the fear. Unfortunately, many children will go on to either emulate that parent as a defense mechanism and continue the cycle of fear or turn away from that parent out of a lack of trust and respect. A child can easily get hurt and traumatized in a darkened closet, an unfamiliar place, or if kept alone in a room with dangerous materials such as a bathroom or shed. At the same time, a child can be frightened if sent to time-out by a parent whose own temper is out of control.

Don't Overuse Time-Out as Your Only Means of Discipline

If time-out is the only plan you have in your parental bag of tricks, it soon loses its effectiveness. For some children, time-out begins to sound like some kind of mantra, "You'll go to time-out . . . you'll go to time-out . . . you'll go to time-out . . ." Like the word no, use time-out sparingly and for situations that call for it.

Send Out a Warning First

If your child is doing something that may warrant a time-out, warn him or her first, and give your child an opportunity to stop or improve the behavior. Of course with toddlers you might have to skip the warning as they are about to pull a lamp onto their head. In that case, act quickly and remove your child from the danger. If your toddler becomes upset, explain simply that he or she was in danger and you understand that he or she is upset. If your child cries for a few moments, allow it. When it's over, hold your child lovingly and remind your child that you want him or her to be safe.

Give a Simple, Clear Explanation for the Time-Out

There is no need to give a speech or enter into a debate. "I asked you to stop pulling the cat's tail because it hurts her and because she could bite you. I told you that if you didn't stop you would go to time-out. You didn't stop pulling the cat's tail, so you are going to time-out."

Follow Through With Time-Out Immediately

You have the best opportunity to teach your child good behaviors when you follow through with time-out immediately. Your child does something wrong, you explain the reason for time-out, and off he goes. Delays create confusion and mixed messages. Toddlers, in particular, will not remember an hour later why they are in time-out. Timing your child out in the evening for something he did in the morning is a complete waste of everybody's time.

Review the Reason for Time-Out With Your Child Afterwards

When your child returns from time-out, spend a few minutes talking about what sent her there in the first place. The talk should be brief and nonthreatening "Why did I send you to time-out? Why is what you did wrong? What would be a better thing to do next time?" This chat can also give your child the chance to redeem herself because it allows her to state what she did and how she knows now it was wrong. Although a toddler probably can't answer these questions and you will have to outline the answers for her, an older child can.

When It's Over . . . Move On

When your child has done the "time" for a misdeed, the event is over. There is no need to berate your child publicly with "You better not do that again or you'll be back in there" or with long-winded lectures. You can even give your child a simple greeting of "We're glad you're back, let's have some fun" along with a hug or a kiss. Remember that you want your child to learn from the experience in order to do the right thing next time.

Ten Reasons Parents Crash and Burn With Time-Out

1. Time-Out is Way Too Long

Sometimes parents get caught in the trap of thinking that the longer their son or daughter is in time-out, the more effective it will be. This could be a problem. When a child's time-out becomes too long, new problems usually surface. For example, a child can become upset or frightened because he or she is alone. Another child kept in time-out too long could create new mischief and new reasons to get into trouble. For both of these scenarios the bottom line is the same: The child has forgotten the original reason he or she was sent to time-out in the first place.

2. The Time-Out Room is the Most Fun Place in the House

Think about it: How uncomfortable could it be to be sent to your room where there are toys, games, a TV, and maybe Nintendo? Besides a child's bedroom should really be a positive, happy place and not a punishment zone.

3. A Parent Keeps Talking to the Child During Time-Out

Time-out means that for a short period of time, a child is going to be alone in a quiet place to calm down or to think over what got him or her in trouble in the first place. Sometimes parents are so exasperated that they cannot leave their little one alone. For example, a child is told to go into time-out and mom follows the child saying, "You know why you're there, right? I'm tired of all of this. Why don't you listen to me?" As long as the mom keeps the conversation going, the child is not in time-out.

4. Shouting Threats But Never Following Through

If mom or dad is to be taken seriously by their children, then there must be follow-through. Warning repeatedly "You're heading for time-out. Don't make me get up" and never carrying out your discipline leads your child to one conclusion and one conclusion only . . . you're a pushover. Use the three-strikes system but at the end of the third warning, act on your words.

5. No Opportunity for the Child to Sit Quietly

Time-out is most effective when a child is in a quiet place. However, sometimes life doesn't afford us that luxury. For example, if you are at a family barbecue and your child needs a little time-out, take your son or daughter around to the side of the house or to some bushes away from the group. Stay with your little one but try not to get into a conversation. Sometimes all you need is a wall or corner to separate you and your child from the crowd until he or she has calmed down.

6. Time-Out is Done in Public in a Demeaning Way

Like all discipline, the purpose of time-out is to help your child learn how to improve his or her behavior in order to do better next time. We've all seen parents in public who are so rattled by their child that they are no longer in control. Soon they're screaming also, or using some kind of frightening voice. The parent creates a spectacle by grabbing the child by the arm and using harsh, unreasonable threats. I recall once hearing a frustrated mom go from saying "Come on dear, behave" one moment to "I am going to beat you within an inch of your life" the next. When a child is demeaned in public, he or she feels embarrassed, confused, or hurt. Instead of remorse, the child frequently experiences anger or a desire to get back at his or her parent. The parent also unwittingly teaches the child that as a parent, he or she doesn't know how to behave either. Take a deep breath and a few moments to calm down, then explain to your child what he or she did wrong, and why.

7. Time-Out is the Only Rabbit in Your Hat

Time-out can be very effective but if overused will lose its effectiveness. Choose those situations that seem most important to you. Often a child will realize he or she is heading for trouble with a simple look from mom or dad and will quickly improve his or her behavior. Other times it may be more appropriate for a child to lose a privilege for a short time or be asked to do something around the house.

8. Using Time-Out Even Though It's Not Effective

Like it or not, not all children respond to time-out. Monitor your child carefully to see if time-out is truly effective or if you are wasting your time. If you believe that after using time-out correctly your child continues to misbehave, it may be wise to conclude that it is not effective. But all is not lost. This just means that as a parent you must determine which form of intervention works best with your child. If your child is articulate, does he or she learn more when permitted to discuss the matter with you? Or would your child benefit from losing a favorite toy or TV show for an hour? No two children are the same, but all can learn from their mom's and dad's guidance.

9. Threatening a Child When He or She Returns From Time-Out

Everyone knows that a child's misbehaving can really test a parent's patience. And some days are definitely worse than

A Creative Twizt on Time-Out: Letting Your Children Time Themzelvez Out

Be flexible and keep your eyes open when it comes to determining what works best with your little one. Some children are able to realize early on that their behavior is out of control or inappropriate and they need to time themselves out. Perhaps all they need is a nod from you or a comment such as, "I think it's that time." In these situations a child has clearly learned the real purpose of time-out: to use a few quiet moments to settle down.

others. But one thing to try to keep in mind is this: When your child has successfully returned from being in time-out, forget about the incident that sent him or her there and move one. Congratulate yourself because your intervention was successful.

10. Forgetting to Give a Warm Greeting When Your Child Successfully Returns From a Time-Out

When your child successfully returns from time-out, he or she always needs encouragement and praise. Praise sends the message that you are glad to see him or her and that you believe the problem is over. With a hug or warm pat you might say, "You're back. Good. Let's have some fun." This allows the child to redeem himself or herself and to put the incident behind everybody.

One More Thing to Keep in Mind

Time-out is a very popular means of disciplining a child. If you opt to use time-out make sure that you use it correctly and safely. Remember that we correct our children so that they might learn from their mistakes and know better what to do next time. And as teachers to our little ones we must always keep in mind that they are always watching us as role models.

Redirection: The Great Toddler Diversion

For children under the age of two, this is one lovely little solution to hold onto. Did you ever notice that children at this age sometimes don't know why they are upset. Explaining it to mom or dad is impossible. Maybe it's because you took out their red sneakers and not their blues ones . . . sometimes there's just no way of knowing for sure. Often the thing that changes a little one's attitude is a diversion. When your little one is fussy in the morning, "Did you pet the doggie this morning? Good morning, doggie." When your little one is restless in a restaurant, "Let's build something with the sugar packets."

The point behind diversion is that you are attempting to shift your child's attention away from the problem and onto something better. Does it work every time? Of course not, but it does work often enough to keep handy when you need it.

One important notion to remember is that diversion is not bribery. Diversion is meant to distract a child into forgetting that he or she is frustrated or upset; bribery is attempting to buy a child's good behavior with food or a toy. Diversion as a

Some Toddler Diversions

+ Point out of the nearest window and say, "Is that a bird sitting on a branch outside?"

+ Grab the closest book or magazine and say, "We haven't read this book in a long time, let's look at it. What beautiful pictures!"

+ Pick up a favorite stuffed animal and say, "Look, I think Pooh Bear wants to dance with us. He says he wants us to sing to him. Twinkle, twinkle . . . "

+ "I bet you can really jump now. Come on, let's see how high you can jump."

technique with very young children, even infants, helps them through those difficult moments in development. Bribery, on the other hand, teaches a child how to be manipulative to get what he or she wants. Unfortunately, bribery often encourages "bratty" behavior.

Advice From Experts in the Front Line

In my experience, I have found that some of the loveliest and most effective interventions for tantrums have come from parents. This discovery only confirms my belief even more — that the parents who use both their intuition and common sense do best with their children. Let me share a handful of homespun interventions that I have stolen from parents over the years.

Do-Over

Stacey and her dad go to the public library to take out a few books. While waiting on line, Stacey begins to misbehave. She doesn't want to wait on line quietly and pushes the boy in front of her. Dad, knowing where this is going, quietly whispers in his daughter's ear, "Let's go outside a minute" and heads for the lobby. Once in the lobby, dad gets down on his knee and look his little girl in the eye. In a gentle voice he says, "You know what, Stacey? I have a feeling that this would be a good time for a do-over. Now I bet if we think really hard, we can figure out what we need to do. Let's look around . . . we're at the library . . . how do people behave at the library?" After a short discussion with his daughter in which he asks for her input, they go back inside. Once on the line, Dad gives his daughter a warm thumbs-up as she eagerly does her do-over.

Do-over is a clever intervention that takes advantage of a young child's desire to be playful. When a little one starts to misbehave or becomes disruptive, mom or dad takes the child aside and whispers, "You know what? I think that we should probably have a do-over."

Do-over can be a fun intervention because:

1. The parent utilizes a quality all children possess in spades — the desire to be playful.
2. The parent removes the child from any public attention and avoids embarrassing him or her and fueling negative attention.
3. The parent asks for the child's ideas and input so that the parent is not telling the child what to do. Instead they are developing a better plan — together.

Role Play

"Okay Emily, tomorrow we're going to have a very special day. We're going to Aunt Susie's wedding. You have a new dress, new shoes, and tomorrow we'll even curl your hair. But let's think for a moment. We're going to be in church. So how should we act when we are in church? I know. We can pretend that you are the beautiful Belle from Beauty and the Beast. Now how would she behave?"

Role play is very similar to do-over because it taps into a child's playfulness, however, it also uses a child's imagination and creativity. Role play is a way of successfully preparing a child for an outing so that when he or she gets there, the child knows exactly what to do. Be creative and pick a favorite character from literature, the movies, or TV that your child knows or admires. Role play how that character would behave in that situation. Now let me add that you should pick a character known for doing the right thing and not for busting up the room. In other words, role playing Winnie the Pooh is a better bet than the Power Rangers or the Three Stooges.

Role Play can be very effective because:

1. Your child is encouraged to be playful and to use his or her imagination.
2. Your child prepares and rehearses for the special event by talking it over with you ahead of time. By creating a mental image in your child's head, he or she knows what to expect and is less likely to be overwhelmed.
3. Using role play the day before allows you to use cues or reminders during the actual event, such as "Belle, you are such a lady today." Simple reminders like this help your little one recall the dress rehearsal and encourage him or her to have fun with the role play.

The next two interventions are not as playful but are just as effective because they allow children to have some control over the consequences of what they have done. Your child plays an active role in deciding whether he or she will be in or out of trouble.

You Choose

Jennifer and mom sit down for lunch at a local deli restaurant. While waiting for their sandwiches to come, Jennifer starts silly at the table. She slides off her chair and tries to sit under the table. Jennifer's mom quietly encourages her to sit up. Without showing her growing agitation, mom gives her daughter the following choices:

"Jennifer, when we are eating at the table, we sit up in our chairs. Look around, see everyone is sitting up. Now you have a choice — you can sit up like the big girl I know you can be and we'll continue having a good time or I can take you to the Ladies Room and time you out. Think it over. You choose."

With this intervention, a child is given a gentle but firm reminder that he or she is sailing into trouble. The child has a choice to a) stop misbehaving or b) receive the consequence. You choose is a type of early warning system that gives a child some responsibility and control over his or her actions and the consequences that follow.

What's important to mention here is that from past experience, Jennifer knows her mom means what she says. The choices are not open for debate and negotiation. Jennifer decides to sit up and behave rather than be timed out in the Ladies Room.

You choose works because:

1. A child is given fair warning that he or she is getting into trouble.
2. The choices are clear and simple with minimal drama on the mother's part.
3. Perhaps most importantly, the child plays an active part in deciding what happens to him or her.

Pick Your Consequences

Michael loved to play on the computer after school. He loved it so much that sometimes his mother couldn't get him off of it — even at dinner time. Their normal routine was that his mother would call him, Michael would yes her to death, and then there would be a big explosion.

One day Michael's mom sat him down to talk this problem over. She told him that she didn't like getting into fights over the computer every day. Michael confessed that he hated being yelled at so much. Michael's mom asked for his help and tossed some questions at him. What did Michael think was a fair amount of time to play on the computer? How should mom warn him that his time was almost up? And lastly, what should happen to Michael if he doesn't get off the computer after the time is up? After some discussion and negotiation, Michael and his mom decided that she would give him two warnings to let him know that his time was almost up. First warning, mom would send the dog into Michael's bedroom as a hint that it was almost time to stop. Second warning, mom would set an egg-timer next to the computer for five minutes to remind him that when the timer went off he was to be off the computer. Michael and his mom put this agreement in writing and posted it on the refrigerator.

If Michael didn't get off the computer after the egg-timer rang he would suffer the following consequences:

1. *Michael would not be allowed to watch his favorite TV show after dinner that night.*
2. *Michael could not play on the computer the next day. This plan worked for a while until one day Michael stayed on the computer after the egg-timer went off. When mom had to dole out the consequences Michael protested loudly. All mom had to do was to point to their written agreement and to remind Michael that he played a key part in deciding what happened to him. This reminder took the steam out of Michael's fight because he had taken an active part in setting up the agreement.*

Very often children will do better if they play an active hands-on role in what happens to them. When encouraged to think, children become more aware of the connection between what they do and the consequences that follow. A child encouraged to think is more apt to do the right thing in other situations or when his or her parent is not around.

This intervention can be used either before a situation develops or afterward. In either case, a child is given some say as to what his or her consequences will be rather than having mom or dad randomly decide or impose what will happen. Pick your consequences is a handy intervention because:

1. Children have a say in what happens to them when they misbehave.
2. The rules and consequences are clear and posted on the refrigerator.
3. The consequences are agreed upon by both the child and the parent.
4. Children learn to associate their behavior with the reality of what will happen if they misbehave. In other words, children learn the lesson of being accountable for their actions.

The Golden Rules of Tantrums

Tantrums are a normal part of your child's development.

Always remember the boy scout's motto: Be prepared.

Never look around at the faces of those people watching you when your child is having a tantrum in public.

The more involved you are with your child's tantrum, the longer it will last.

Remember to catch your child being good as often as you can.

Understand that all children want their parents' love and attention.

Move on and forget about the tantrum once it is over. It's history.

Chapter 3

Everybody's Favorites: The Supermarket and the Restaurant

The Supermarket

Oh, that trip to the supermarket. One never knows how things will turn out. When your little one is in good spirits, the trip is easy and routine. But when he or she melts down into that little tantrum person, you feel as if you're being followed through the store by a 10,000-watt searchlight, "We know who you are lady. We can hear that screaming kid all the way in produce." In your own experience how many moms and dads have you seen with that look of desperation and exasperation on their faces? Plenty, I'm sure. How many times have *you* been that mom or dad? It's okay.

Ka Boom! The Supermarket Tantrum

A few years ago, a mom came to my office very upset over an incident that occurred at the supermarket with her son. Her four year old had wanted some candy and mom said no. His reaction was to cry and scream at the very top of his lungs. Feeling very embarrassed and not sure what to do, the mom

Supermarket Do's and Don'ts

Do	Don't
Bring your children when they are relaxed, rested, and fed.	Bring your children to the supermarket when they are tired, hungry, or both.
Bring a list and know exactly what you need.	Do "major" shopping during busy store hours.
Pick quiet store hours to shop.	Take your little one food shopping after they have spent the day at school or a major activity.
Ask your child to be your helper: marking off the list, spotting the items on a shelf, pulling the coupons.	Let your young children run through the store unsupervised where you cannot see them.
Bring an activity bag to keep your child entertained when he or she grows fidgety.	Get into the habit of buying items you don't need but your child demands.
Bring a healthy snack from home or pick one out with your child, for example: bottled water, raisins, pretzels.	Get in the habit of letting your children have candy bars and little toys at the check-out counter. It's best if you never get into that habit.
Turn shopping into an opportunity to learn: how many kinds of fruits can you name? What animals give us meat?	

tried to talk her son out of this developing tantrum. His screams escalated and he started to hit his mother. Now very frustrated and near tears herself, she picked him up. With that the little boy bit his mother hard on her breast. She saw stars and, feeling defeated, gave in and handed him the candy bar.

Now this mom knew that giving in to her son all but guaranteed another such episode in the future, but the situation overwhelmed her. She wanted to be prepared for the next time. Here are a few of the solutions we discussed:

Try to Get Ahead of the Tantrum, and Intervene Before It Happens. How?

Use Distraction. Distraction means diverting your child's attention away from the thing he or she is currently focused on. For example, if your little one is fixated on a bag of chocolate chip cookies in the cookie aisle, you might try, "Let's go see what kind of fish are in the fish department today. Maybe they even have real lobsters!" or "Look. Look. All this fruit! There are so many shapes and colors."

Use Diversion. Diversion means not only taking your child's attention away from the thing he or she is focused upon, but also changing the activity. For example, "Can you help me? Would you hold mom's food list. I need a good helper." And if your child is old enough, "Here, you can cross off the list everything we find in the store." Or . . . you can reach into your pocketbook or activity bag and give your child something to play with or scribble on. Or . . . hand your child a healthy snack, "Um, let's have a good snack. So delicious." And ignore the request for candy.

But When the Tantrum Happens Anyway . . . First try to ignore it, and don't make any attempt to talk your child out of it. Appeals such as, "Come on, no crying in the store" will only send your child into a tantrum that much faster. Remember too, that some tantrums are short-lived, lasting for just a few seconds. They are really more of a protest and quickly fade when something or someone catches your child's attention. If you're lucky and the tantrum quickly disappears, kiss your child and say, "You know what? It's fun to shop with you."

If you find yourself in the midst of a full-blown tantrum and there's no underground shelter to hide in, try the following suggestions.

Look for a quiet place in the store, one that is out of the

way of the public eye such as a restroom or empty aisle. If no such place exists in the store, consider leaving your cart and taking your son or daughter out to the car. You could tell a clerk that you should be back in just a few moments and that if you are not back in 20 minutes then it's okay to empty it. If you elect to talk to a store clerk about your cart, do it with as little drama as possible. Remember, tantrums feed on attention so if you lose your cool, things are certain to get worse.

Once in a quiet place or out in the car, you might say something to your child like the following, "Let me tell you what's happening Billy. It is not okay to scream or yell in the store. And it is never okay to hit mommy. We will sit here quietly until you feel better and then we will finish our shopping. I really need you to be my helper today." At this point you should take your attention away from your child. You might busy yourself with something in your wallet or just look out the window if that's all that's available. Your child will try to steer your attention back to himself or herself but doing so only keeps the tantrum going. So resist.

When the tantrum passes, wait a few moments for your child to stop crying and settle down. Then hug your child and get back to shopping. If your little one manages to behave the rest of the time in the store, then plan to do a little something special either on the way home or once you are at home. Maybe it's just sitting for a few minutes before emptying the grocery bags and sharing some juice and a snack. If your child was good, tell him or her. And even if your child's behavior was shaky at best, find one little thing to praise. Children always want their mom and dad's approval.

There are Some Children Whose Tantrums Can Be Frightening Because They Become Physically Aggressive.   Children can throw some of their best tantrums in a public place. Why's that? My hunch is that one of the reasons is because their parents react differently in public. A public tantrum can be terribly embarrassing and unnerving.

When Tantrums May Require Professional Help

1. If your child's tantrums have escalated to physical attacks against him or herself, other people, pets, or objects.

2. If you notice a dramatic change in your child's personality and throwing a tantrum is very out of character.

3. If you find that you cannot control your own temper in reaction to your child's tantrums.

4. If, in spite of your intervention, your child's tantrums increase in frequency, intensity, and duration.

For a brief moment you might find yourself thinking, "Is this my kid?" Strangers are usually staring and some may even toss a wisecrack your way. In your urgency to quiet the tantrum, you may actually be doing more to set it off. As you fight with the tantrum, it mushrooms into an ugly scene for everyone. Sometimes a child in the midst of a full-blown tantrum will react physically. Perhaps he or she will push you away or try to slap or even bite you. In that case, it's best to take physically aggressive children out to the car to avoid them injuring themselves or somebody else. If the tantrum doesn't start to wind down after 20 or 25 minutes, take your child home and use time-out. You might say, "I can see that you're having a lot of trouble calming down. We are going home now and you will have time-out until you can pull yourself together."

Remember, Often a Child's Tantrums Will Become Worse Before They Get Better. That's because children want to see if you're really serious and mean what you say. How many times have you heard a parent say, "My child's testing me"? Even young toddlers can figure out which parent means what they say and which one is the "softy." When you first begin to intervene with your child's tantrums you may notice that the first time worked very well, but the next two or three times did not. The first time was successful because your child was probably caught off guard. The element of surprise was enough to change the behavior and snuff out the tantrum. But the next few times may not go as well because your son or daughter wants to see if you really mean what you say or do. Those tantrums may even appear worse, more intense, and actually last longer. But don't lose heart, because if you can manage to stand your ground and be consistent, the tantrums will go away.

Restaurants

Did you ever notice the expressions on the faces of waitresses or waiters when you bring young children into the restaurant? Usually the reaction is mixed — happy expressions and that look of "Please don't seat them in my station." As a waitress going through college, I was one those people mumbling that very sentiment under my breath. There are a few reasons for this attitude. As fun as eating out in a restaurant can be, many young children have a tendency to misbehave. And parents, being driven crazy by their children, have a tendency to drive their waiter or waitress crazy.

Even though it feels like a hundred years ago when I was a waitress, I can still recall quite vividly several episodes with children. I can remember one instance in which a couple who were regulars to the restaurant brought their two children under five in at the height of a busy Saturday night. After waiting 45 minutes for their table, the two little ones started acting out. When I got to the table, one of the parents asked me to quick go into the kitchen and bring out a chocolate cream pie. When I returned, they immediately sent me back for some French fries, then baked clams, and then sodas — one at a time. By the time I could get their dinner order, their table was filled with desserts, sodas, and appetizers. I was so backed up with my other tables that I didn't know if I was coming or going. Needless to say, the children never settled down and my service was terrible.

On yet another occasion, I watched in dismay as a toddler was allowed to rip open all the sugar packets, take the tops off the salt and pepper shakers, put food in her milk, and throw all her vegetables on the floor. When the little girl started using a broccoli spear as a crayon on the wall, I thought I would truly lose it. I remember thinking to myself, why is this child allowed to behave in ways that would never be tolerated at home?

Dining out can be a lot of fun for everyone, including the staff but the table below outlines a few key things to keep in mind before you go:

Restaurant Do's and Don'ts

Do	Don't
Dine during quiet or off-peak hours.	Bring your chidren to a restaurant where the "expected dining behavior" is beyond their understanding or maturity level.
Discuss good restaurant behavior with your children before dining out, and accept no less.	
Choose restaurants that are "kid friendly" and can serve your family without long delays between courses.	Bring your children to a crowded restaurant during peak hours or when you know there will be a long wait.
Always bring an activity box. And if you have forgotten, ask the restaurant if they have crayons and coloring placements. Some restaurants even have their own activity boxes.	Allow your children to throw food, dismantle centerpieces, or destroy condiments.
	Allow little ones to run freely through a restaurant unsupervised. Restaurants can be busy, dangerous places for young children.
Bring along a healthy, light snack such as raisons or Cheerios in case there's a wait.	Forget that there are other paying customers who also deserve to enjoy their meal.
Ask your waitress what can be served quickly to your child.	Send your waiter or waitress into the kitchen a hundred times. Make clear requests and remember that your server is human too.
Remove your child from the dining room if he or she starts to scream or become disruptive to the other customers.	Assume that everyone else will think your child's screaming or misbehavior is cute and adorable.

Duck! The Restaurant Tantrum

Restaurant tantrums, like the supermarket and the airplane tantrum, seem to have the same impact on people — like fingernails across a blackboard. Everyone around turns to look, some shake their heads and roll their eyes, and if it's a particularly good tantrum, some people will even ask to change their tables. Away from the screaming child, naturally. I've seen one or two tantrums that actually brought a busy restaurant to a grinding halt for a moment or two.

A restaurant tantrum is similar to a tantrum in a supermarket. The only exception is that there are people around you who are paying to dine out. If your little one starts to unravel at the table, well, they are paying for that as well.

Start out your trip to the restaurant by being prepared. Bring along an activity bag or a few small toys your child will enjoy. Bring along two or three light snacks and a favorite drink. Don't forget to include a sippy cup and some kid-sized utensils. A toddler with an adult-sized restaurant fork can be a scary sight. Talk about where you are going and how everyone is going to behave. Kids do better when they know what is expected of them. If your child is old enough, you might want to play pretend that you are a particular family from a story going out to eat. Talk in the car about how they would act in a restaurant.

If your child starts to fuss, look for things to distract or divert his or her attention. If you're desperate, just stacking sugar packets can do the trick. If there's a little time before your meal comes out, take your child for a walk because sitting in a booster seat or high chair can get uncomfortable and boring.

If it looks as if your child is heading for a tantrum or even just a screaming episode, it's best to remove him or her to a quiet place. As these situations usually occur just as the meal is being served, you may have to take turns eating. Ask the kitchen to keep your food warm while you walk outside or take your child into the restroom. Sometimes just the momentary change in scenery is enough to put a cap on a tantrum and you'll be able to return to the table.

If it looks as if your child has reached the point of no return, you may want to cut your losses, get doggie bags, and head for home. Once home, figure out where you might have gone wrong: Did you eat too late? Was the wait too long? Service too slow? Did you forget to bring something to entertain your child? Knowing what stirred up the tantrum and being prepared beforehand ensures the chances of a pleasant evening next time.

What to Know Before Going to a Restaurant

Picking a Restaurant

When picking a place to eat out with children, consider restaurants that are "kid friendly." Now that's not to say that you should only take your children to fast-food restaurants. But a restaurant that prides itself on offering the public a dining "experience" may not be right for a child. The service may be intentionally slow so that customers can select a bottle of wine, browse leisurely through the menu, and then enjoy each course of their meal. This is delightful if you are having an evening out without the kids but bringing them to such a place could prove hard work for you and everyone around you. Save these lovely spots for when the two of you can be alone or out with friends.

A kid-friendly restaurant knows how to accommodate children. The waiter or waitress knows to get something from the kitchen quick, sometimes without you even asking. Often the hostess will have crayons and paper, and sometimes they even have their own activity box — you just need to ask.

Bring an Activity Box

Service can be unpredictable in any restaurant so it's best to come prepared with something to entertain your children. Why get stuck hunting deep into your pocketbook or looking on the table for anything to occupy your child until the food comes? Even the best-behaved child is on a timer when out in a restaurant. As you wait to be seated, wait to give your order, and wait to be served, your child is tick-tick-ticking away. (See page 11 for activity box ideas.)

Don't Let Children Roam Around a Restaurant Unless You Are With Them

A restaurant can be very stimulating for a child and very dangerous. Waiters are moving about with trays of food, doors are swinging open and shut, strange new sounds are coming from the kitchen, and there's a lot of neat things to touch. It must also be one of Murphy's Laws that if there is something available to injure a child, he or she will go right for it. I saved more than one child from being flattened by a swinging kitchen door.

When Children Come Out to Eat They Should Bring Their Best Behavior With Them

Even though you may not know the person, family, or corporation that owns the restaurant you're dining in and they don't know you, it's important to keep in mind that a restaurant is someone else's property. When children are allowed to be destructive in a restaurant by drawing on the walls, dismantling the centerpieces, or even taking things home, they are not learning how to respect the things in this world that don't belong to them.

Try Not to Torture Your Waiter With a Hundred Trips into the Kitchen

Restaurant folks work on timing. Starting a new table, getting drinks, and placing orders in the kitchen depend on a waiter's ability to time and pace him or herself. An experienced waiter on a packed weekend night can make the job look simple but one over-demanding table can throw a kink into the whole evening. A waiter can be your friend if you work with him or her. When your waiter approaches the table, explain what you will need during the course of the meal for your child. If you need something served to you quickly or special ordered, now is the time to tell the waiter.

Chapter 4

Planez, Trainz, and Automobilez

Did you jump ahead and come to this chapter first? I thought so. So you're the one on the plane with the screaming baby. Of all the tantrums a child could have, I think that most people would unanimously agree that a tantrum on a plane is the worst. There you are wedged in an undersized seat, your little one's screams are so loud that they're interfering with the airport's control tower, and you have no place to go. And the plane hasn't even taken off yet. You see the look on the stewardess' face and know exactly what she's thinking, "I need this screaming kid like I need a hole in my head." Take heart, there are things a parent can do to make a trip on a plane, or even a train or automobile much easier.

I've heard plenty of parents say that they won't travel with their children. They are afraid that they won't be able to handle a tantrum at 30,000 feet or speeding along the railway or interstate. That's too bad because parents are really denying themselves the opportunity to get away and enjoy new places with their children. Remember that I've mentioned before that the secret to success when handling tantrums is to be as a boy scout, go prepared. A mom or dad who has prepared and brought along the necessary diversions for their children goes into the situation feeling confident and ready.

Recently I had the experience of sitting behind a young mom and her two small boys on a plane. The flight was about three hours long and this mom had brought nothing to keep her sons occupied. Curious and fidgety from the onset, the two were ripping the seats apart and beating each other up after a little while. Then the real trouble started. One of the boys started pulling the woman's hair in front of him. Can you imagine the rest of this scenario? The biggest problem here was that these kids were bored and had nothing to do. If only their mom had brought along some coloring books, a snack, and a game or two, the situation would have been a lot more fun for everyone.

Planes

Since nearly everyone has either been guilty of bringing a screaming baby onto a plane or had the great pleasure of sitting behind one, we'll take a look at what to do on an airplane first. To make your journey a smooth one, there is some basic flight information to be aware of as well as some commonsense methods for planning a better trip.

When to Fly

When traveling with a young child it is wise to travel at off-peak hours whenever you can. Off-peak can vary with different airlines but for most it is Monday afternoon through Thursday late morning. The plane is likely to be less crowded and you may even find an empty seat next to you. In general, the flight crew is more relaxed and better able to handle your needs should you require some assistance with your child.

If you are traveling with a baby, the flight you choose should coincide with the baby's sleep schedule. If your baby naps in the afternoon, then picking an afternoon flight would be a good idea. Once settled into your seats, a sleepy baby will most likely drift off into his or her nap. Night flights are also a good idea for babies or older children.

Although not always possible, ask your travel agent to book a nonstop flight when traveling by plane. It's hard enough to get on a plane with children and carry-on luggage without having to repeat this drill a few hours later at another airport. It's disruptive to your children and exhausting for you.

Be Smart and Make Reservations Early

Before children entered your life, it really didn't matter what flights you chose or even when. You could book a spur-of-the moment flight and just go. It wasn't that important where your seat was, no less what delicious meals would be served to you. Most of the time you rolled with the punches because getting to your destination was really the only important thing. If you want to be smart, you will take a different approach when traveling with kids.

Whenever possible, purchase your tickets early . Ask your travel agent or reservationist which airlines offer a wide-body plane like a 747 or a DC-10. The aisles are wider, there's more room to walk around, and they are more apt to show an in-flight movie.

Usually, an early reservation allows you to pick better seats and to have your boarding passes mailed ahead to you. Many travelers like to reserve the bulkhead seats because there is significantly more leg room. A bulkhead seat gives you more room to change diapers if necessary and allows your child some space to play with small toys. There are some definite negatives to the bulkhead seats to be aware of: there's no underseat storage, the arm rests don't move, the food trays can be awkward, and if there's a movie, you'll be about two inches from the screen.

Ask about the menu for your flight when making the reservations. Today many airlines serve only a light snack for short flights. You could be in for trouble if you were counting on the airline meal to entertain your child. Sometimes an airline will serve only a bag of peanuts and a beverage for a snack. This is a problem for a hungry child and dangerous for children two years and under. Other times an airline will serve something that your little one has no desire to eat. Ask about the "special" meals that will be offered during that flight. Some airlines offer fruit plates, cheese and crackers, vegetarian snacks, and kosher meals. If it appeals to you, reserve a meal ahead of time. You are not at your mother's house, so once on the plane it is too late to ask for special food services. When you know what the meal will be, plan accordingly. Bring some of your child's favorite snacks and include a drink or two.

It's Not Necessary to Drag All that Stuff Through the Airport

How many times have you witnessed those poor parents running through the airport dragging a car seat, stroller, baby bags, carry-on luggage, and their children? Please. Travel does not have to be that difficult. On this subject you have two better options: curbside check-in or rent it when you reach your destination.

Curbside check-in allows you to get rid of everything before entering the terminal. Just make sure that you put name tags on everything and that you haven't checked anything you might need on the flight. Keep the kids' snacks, toys, diapers, and "blankies" in a separate carry-on bag. It is also a good idea to keep your own carry-on bag with essentials like cameras, jewelry, medications, and contact lenses. It's Murphy's Law that at some point in your traveling experience, you will reach your destination and your bags will not.

Renting a car seat, stroller, or anything else related to babies is another option to consider when traveling. The rental fees for baby equipment are reasonable in most places. If you will be renting a car you can reserve a car seat. If you will be needing a stroller, high chair, crib, or play pen, you can rent from local rental companies near the hotel or your relatives' home. Many hotels keep cribs and high chairs on hand. Again, it is a good idea to do all this in advance.

Don't Scrimp on Your Child's Safety

Many, many times you will see parents holding their young children on their laps during a flight. In addition to the child getting fidgety and the parent feeling confined in an already too-small space, there is another, more important concern. Think about this for a moment: As the plane heads down the runway for take-off, all the passengers and the flight crew are securely strapped into their seats. Everyone, that is, except the child on the parent's lap. In the event of an emergency or unexpected turbulence, there is a real danger that this child could get injured.

Although buying a seat for your child is an additional expense, your child's safety has no price tag. If you are traveling with an infant or a child who requires a car seat at home, the airlines will allow you to bring your own car seat on board at no extra charge. But you cannot assume there will be an open seat for your child if you do not purchase one ahead of time. If you wait, and there's no seat, the flight crew will have to check the car seat in as luggage.

With you in one seat and your child in another, there's a greater possibility of a pleasant flight for everyone. You have your own space to move about and to assist your child with whatever he or she might need. Your child is no longer fidgeting on your lap getting bored, overheated, and frustrated.

Remember, a contented child is less likely to throw a tantrum during the flight.

Act Like a Boy Scout and Go Prepared

No, traveling with children will never be as easy as traveling alone, but if you are prepared ahead of time, it can be fun. If you can, devote one of the carry-on bags completely to your child and keep it under your seat. That way you will know where everything is and you won't have to climb over other passengers during the flight.

Most importantly, pack the essentials first: extra diapers, wipes, sippy-cup, utensils, and bibs. Remember to toss in a small blanket in case the plane is cold. Bring an extra set of clothes in the event that your child spills something or worse. Next, pack some healthy snacks like fruit and salt-free pretzels. Include something to drink should the airplane not have what your little one likes. Try to avoid candy and snacks high in sugar as these things are not likely to soothe an active child. If you bring something along that has to be microwaved the flight crew can probably be helpful. Keep in mind, however, that the crew must serve the other passengers first and you will have to wait.

Include in your child's carry-on bag some fun toys to play with. Bring a variety of things such as small books, coloring books, finger puppets, puzzles, and a favorite stuffed animal. Your little one will be delighted if you include a surprise toy or two. Wrap it like a gift and let your son or daughter have some fun opening it up. The other passengers will be infinitely thankful if you leave home anything that beeps, barks, or chirps. See the Boredom Busters section on page 79 for some creative ideas.

The Worst: Tantrums on the Plane

Sometimes no matter what lengths you have gone to ensure a happy flight, your child loses it and has a tantrum. Maybe the plane is hot or overcrowded. Maybe your child doesn't feel good or perhaps he or she just doesn't like to fly. It happens. As a parent, you are miserable because now you have a three-alarmer on your hands. The other passengers look at each other and grumble. If you're real lucky, a passenger may even pass a snide remark loud enough for you to hear.

Never Look or Listen to the People Sitting Around You

This is a golden rule of tantrums (see page 52). Tantrums can be unpleasant enough without tuning in to the looks and comments from neighboring passengers. Right from the beginning, tune them out and focus on you and your child. You're a good parent, you've done all the right preparations, there is no reason to feel humiliated as well. There isn't a person on that plane who hasn't been in a similar predicament, even if it was their own tantrums they were contending with.

Keep Distractions Close By

Sometimes you are lucky enough to see the tantrum coming before it arrives. You might want to perfect the ability to head off a tantrum as it can save a lot of aggravation in the long run. When you sense trouble brewing, distractions can work like a charm. By distractions, I mean diverting your little one's attention away from the thing that is causing the problem and onto something that will help him or her to forget about it. If your child seems fidgety, then change the activity — offer a snack, sing a song, play peek-a-boo, or bring out a surprise.

Find Your Patience and Hold Onto It

The last thing your child's tantrum needs to be fueled by is your own tantrum. Sure, tantrums can push a lot of buttons, but if you want tantrums to stop, stay cool. When you lose your temper, your child's tantrum will certainly escalate and your temper may even frighten an out-of-control child. Remember, stay calm. Like everything else, this too shall pass.

Take Your Child to a Quiet Place on the Plane

The problem with airplanes is that they are a confined space; there are only so many places a parent can take a child. But there are two: the lavatories and the very back of the plane.

Tantrums are best dealt with when ignored, but airplane travel does not provide that option. Unlike libraries or supermarkets, once on a plane, you cannot get off. When you cannot ignore the tantrum, take your child to one of these quiet locations on the plane. Most children will not walk during a tantrum so it is best to not drag your little one down the aisle. Once again, this will only fuel the tantrum further. Pick your child up and carry them to the closest available spot. Because planes have a tendency to bounce, you should hold onto your child to avoid injury. Remember, traveling by air is a big event for most people, especially children. Many children become over-saturated by the "newness" of the experience. When they lose control they need to be comforted and soothed.

Although it may not be necessary to say what I am about to say, stay with your child during the tantrum. Don't take a child to the back of the plane or to a lavatory and force him or her to sit in time-out. An unattended child on an airplane can be dangerous, especially in a cramped lavatory. Instead, distract your child by looking at all the knobs and compartments, "Look Matthew, you have to push this button to make the water in the sink go away." Talk about all the things your child will see and do when you arrive, "Today's going to be fun. We're going to a hotel. There's a great big bed and even a television."

Traveling by Automobile

Traveling by car is an integral part of our daily lives. We drive to work, the store, visit friends, and go on vacation. Automobile tantrums don't just appear when you are zooming down the highway on a cross-country trip. No sir, these tantrums can appear during your Saturday morning routine, or any time at all. But unlike airplanes, in which you are dramatically limited during a tantrum, automobiles offer many more options.

Day-to-Day Driving

In today's society, we are constantly in motion. We shuttle kids here and there and try to tackle 100 errands at a time. Everybody, including our children, can get stressed out. The following are a few pointers to make daily driving more enjoyable and safer.

Know Where You Are Going Beforehand and Plan Accordingly

Once again, jumping into your car and just going is not as easy when you have children. Just ask any parent who has taken his or her child from a car seat half a dozen times in one day. Although most children love the idea of getting in the car and going somewhere with mom and dad, the novelty can wear thin. It may be a good idea to keep an activity bag in the car that contains books and toys to entertain your children should you decide to make one more stop or take the scenic route home. Before leaving the house, take a few snacks that are easy to get to and you can pass to your children. Think about bringing a favorite tape or CD. In this way, you have some backup should your child grow tired of being strapped in the back seat.

Don't Neglect Safety, Even if You Are Just Going On a Short Errand

A few years ago, I had dubious opportunity to witness the importance of children wearing their seat belts. While sitting at a red light, I watched as two cars crashed into each other head on. Fortunately for everyone neither car was going very fast, and no one was seriously hurt. However, one of the cars contained several children, and none of them were in a seatbelt, no less a car seat. As if watching a slow motion picture, I saw the children become projectiles as they flew from the back seat, crashing into the front dashboard. In an instant, they were thrown from their seats without any means to protect themselves. It was a miracle no one was seriously hurt. But what I witnessed made a lasting impression. When I see parents on the road and their children are unrestrained in the car, I am very tempted to approach them to say, "Excuse me, but are you crazy?"

Before you pull away from the curb, make sure everyone is securely strapped into their seats. I know that it is tempting to hold a young infant in your arms rather than putting him or her into a car seat or to allow a tired child to lay his or her head on your lap rather than be in a seat belt. But a child is never safer in your arms than in a car seat or seat belt. Most accidents occur close to home when someone is just running out for that quart of milk or running to pick the kids up from baseball. Countless adults and children are injured or killed because they were not properly restrained. The statistics are alarming.

Refereeing From the Front Seat Can Be Dangerous Business

A screaming child, or worse, fighting siblings can be torture when you are driving. It can be nearly impossible to resist turning around and reaching into the back seat to break it up.

But when you take your eyes off the road and turn around to the back, nobody is driving the car. Not good.

If your baby or toddler is in the back screaming, you have a few options: wait for a red light or pull to the side to pass back a snack or toy; toss a favorite lullaby into the cassette player; ignore them; or head for home. Maybe you are trying to cover too much territory or accomplish too many errands in one day and your little one is saying, "Mom, enough!"

Older children fighting in the back seat can be maddening. After a little while everyone is agitated and screaming, especially you. If your verbal reprimands from the front seat are ignored, it is probably time to pull the car over and hand out the consequences. Before pulling the car over, you might give the two wrestlers in the back one final warning, "When I pull this car over, you both will be punished. I don't care who started what. Figure it out between the two of you fast and settle down now." Many times arguing siblings will only listen when they realize that mom is pulling off the road. If that is the case, resist the temptation to give in. You should dole out the consequences anyway. The kids had their warning but decided not to take you seriously. Your consequences should be fair and something you can carry out soon, for example, no television today after dinner.

Family Vacation

With the cost of airline tickets and train fares, many families opt to vacation by car. Vacationing by car can be fun because you can stop when you want, take the routes you like, and get to see more of the country. Being prepared and planning ahead will make your family's trip more pleasant and memorable.

Keep What You May Need on Hand in the Car

If you are planning a long road trip with a child, take some time to know what you might need in the car. It's a good idea

Surprize . . . Surprize

Whether traveling by plane, train, or automobile take along a few wrapped presents to surprise your child. Look in the dollar stores because they often have inexpensive toys and books for children.

Wrap up the presents with some extra bright-colored paper you may have lying around the house. At different times during your trip surprise your child with a present. It works wonders.

to pack an activity bag that contains favorite books, small toys, and games. For your own sanity, try to leave most of the "noisemakers" at home and instead bring toys that engage your child's curiosity. Don't forget a favorite stuffed animal and blanket for naps and cuddling. Bring along a few surprises that your child can open up along the way.

When traveling by car you might consider bringing a cooler along. You can fill it with snacks and drinks and maybe a few surprises too. Coolers are also handy because they allow you to bring a little something extra for the hotel or motel.

When Vacationing, Don't Try to Break Any Speed or Mileage Records

Every minute counts when you are on vacation but asking young children to stay put for hours at a time can be asking too much. Plan your trip with frequent stops and be flexible if you have to stop before a specific destination. Often all a young child needs is a few minutes to stretch his or her legs or to have a fresh diaper change. Today, fast-food restaurants like McDonalds provide playground areas for children. Pull over, get yourself a cool drink, and let your children climb the monkey bars for a little while. You will all be much happier later.

Shift People Around in the Car

Everyone can get stiff and grouchy during a long road trip. During one of your rest stops, shift family members around so that everyone gets a different view. For little ones in car seats who cannot be moved, don't worry. Very often a young child will enjoy that a different person is in the back seat with them to play or read them a story.

Watch for Clues That Your Child is Reaching the End of His or Her Fuse

Even the best little road travelers reach a point when they are bored, achy from sitting, hungry or tired. You can often see and hear the clues: whining, restlessness, demanding. Take this opportunity to surprise with something, offer a snack, or consider a short rest stop.

If your little one has reached the point of no return, scolding or losing your temper is a waste of time. While some young ones can cry themselves to sleep, others can carry on for a very long time. If stopping is not an option because of your location or time of day, then choose a mellow station on the radio and hang in there. Focus on your driving and the music. Driving faster or getting overly involved with the backseat tirade is dangerous for everyone.

Trains

Although the cost can be prohibitive, most children love to travel by train. They love the chug-chug-chugging of the big locomotive and being able to watch as stores, houses, and trees whiz by. A family vacation by train like those that run through the Canadian Rockies is a thrill for everyone to remember.

However, like airline travel, you are in a confined space. It is a good idea to be prepared and know what you are getting into.

Make Your Reservations Early and Travel Off-Peak

Plan a trip with your travel agent well in advance. Ask for brochures and any relevant information to make the experience more pleasant. Having your tickets ahead of time allows you to avoid the madness of the train ticket counters and waiting in long lines. Make sure about seating arrangements from your travel agent so that you can be assured of sitting together or having a good seat. At this time, inquire about meals on board the train and the hours of dining service. Plan to bring your own snacks in case the menu fails to excite your child. Traveling during off-peak hours typically means that the train should be less crowded.

 Just like the airlines, you are permitted to bring car seats on board a train for your child's added protection.

Introduce Yourself to One of the Porters or Conductors and Become Familiar With the Layout of the Train

Ask a porter or conductor to explain where the bathrooms are, hours of dining, cars you can visit. Don't be afraid to ask for their assistance when moving through the train or between cars.

Keep Safety in Mind When on Board a Train

While trains can be a very exciting way to travel, they also have their dangers. Trains bounce and lurch and often stop suddenly. Hold onto your children's hand when walking down the aisles. Keep older children closely supervised to avoid the temptation of getting too close to dangers like changing cars or pressing buttons.

Tantrums on the Train

Airplanes and trains are very similar; both are confined spaces with little availability for privacy. But should your little one have a tantrum while on board the train, I suggest that you follow the same suggestions as presented in the airplane section of this chapter: Find a quiet place to take your child, and soothe him or her until the problem subsides.

Boredom Busters

One of the things I stress in this book is the importance of being prepared when going out or traveling with your children. By being prepared, I mean that you ought to always have activities and snacks that can entertain your children should the need arise. And believe me, the need will arise, because tantrums never surface at a good time. No . . . tantrums occur when you're circling 40,000 feet over O'Hare Airport or when you're caught in bumper to bumper traffic at rush hour.

As for me, I travel with an activity bag for my son in the back seat of the car. In it I keep a variety of things: a bag of pretzels, diapers, wipes, baby-size spoon and fork, and a menagerie of little toys. What's important about the toys is that they don't come in the house, therefore, my son only plays with them when we are out. He doesn't see them all the time. When I see that a toy has lost its magic, I know that it's time to replace it.

Look through my list of suggestions and feel free to steal one or all of them. I know from experience that a good activity is always worth stealing. You will notice that many of the things that entertain small children are right inside your home. For example, small cardboard jewelry boxes. Toddlers love to take the lids off and put stuff inside and then take it out.

Children three years and under:

+ hand and finger puppets
+ measuring spoons
+ 6-inch soft bendable rulers
+ deck of cards
+ small books with pop-ups, moveable parts, and finger puppets*
+ hand-held mirror
+ blocks
+ washable crayons
+ coloring book
+ index cards
+ pipe cleaners
+ jar of bubbles — for outside use only
+ simple wooden jigsaw puzzles
+ small cardboard gift boxes or small plastic containers
+ plastic toothbrush or soap case
+ calculator* — toddlers love to bang away at the numbers, plus it's a great way to learn numbers.
+ stop watch* — toddlers love to listen to the ticking sound and watch the needle move around the dial.
+ egg-timer* — toddlers love it when the bell rings.
+ store catalogs
+ mini flashlight* — Buy only those appropriately marked for children three and under. Toddlers enjoy

* Parents: Please note that some of the activities have an asterisk * next to them. The * indicates that this toy or object requires your supervision because it contains small pieces that young children might put in their mouths.

turning it on and off and pointing the beam of light at objects.
+ mini photo album — organize a small photo album with photographs of your child that are funny or memorable.
+ children's sunglasses
+ funny hats
+ small stuffed animal*
+ musical toys*
+ manipulatives with different shapes, sizes, colors, and textures

Children three to five years:

+ workbooks
+ comic books
+ puzzles — keep the pieces together in a plastic container
+ activity boxes — created and designed by your child with his or her favorite things inside
+ costume jewelry*
+ books on tape
+ rubics cube
+ deck of cards
+ activity books
+ musical instrument — for car travel
+ Leggos
+ blocks

Children ages five and over:

+ electronic and computer games
+ checkers
+ bingo

- Chutes and Ladders
- Barrel of Monkeys
- chess
- Junior Scrabble
- travel journal — to record the family's vacation
- tape recorder
- disposable pocket camera
- puzzles and brainteasers
- maps
- compass
- Etch-a-Sketch
- foreign language tapes and workbooks

Not Sure What is Safe For your Child?

- Consumer Product Safety Commission (CPSC): (800) 638-CPSC

- *The Best Toys, Books, Videos, and Software for Kids 1997:* Joanne Oppenheim & Stephanie Oppenheim, Prima Publishing, Rocklin, CA.

Other Valuable Resources for Traveling with Children

- *Trouble-Free Travel with Children* (1996): Vicki Lansky. Deephaven, MN: Book Peddlers. A light-hearted book filled with activities for families on the go.
- *Merrily We Roll Along:* offered by the National Association for the Education of Young Children, 1509 Sixteenth Street NW, Washington, D.C., 20036-1426, (202) 232-8777. This brochure describes ideas for keeping kids happy while in their car seats.

- *Miles of Smiles* (1993): Carole Terwillinger Meyers. Albany,CA: Carousel Press. Book contains games and activities for children ages four and up.
- *Travel Games for Kids* (1992): Andrew Langley. Lee, MA: Berkshire House. Book contains word play, puzzles, and hand games for children ages four and up.
- *Kids' Travel: A Backseat Survival Kit* (1994): Palo Alto, CA: Klutz Press. This book is packed with fun activities, games, and brainteasers for children ages seven and up.

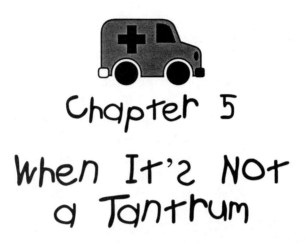

Chapter 5

When It's Not a Tantrum

Okay, I survived my first tantrum. Then the second and the third. I learned to redirect my son. I learned to ignore staring strangers. I can relax, I thought. I've got it all under control. Oh, how naive we parents can be! A few weeks after "my first tantrum," I told my son he couldn't climb on the sofa with his shoes on. He promptly propelled himself to the floor in a swan dive. (Thank goodness for thick carpeting!) Then he started holding his breath. For longer than I can! He turned beet red. I was in the next phase of parenting. When a tantrum is not a tantrum!

Breath Holding

Roughly 5% of children will hold their breath when angry or upset. Watching your child intentionally hold his breath, turn blue, and pass out is an experience most of us would not like to have.

Fortunately, because breathing is a function of our automatic nervous system, we can't just stop breathing when we feel like it. Therefore once a child passes out, he or she will automatically resume breathing.

Recently I bumped into a preschool director who told me that her son does this very thing. She said that he usually holds his breath during a tantrum. The first time it happened, the preschool director said that she wasn't sure what was going on. She saw her son on the floor, walked over to him, and noticed that he had turned blue. That image nearly scared her to death. A second or two later he started to breath and his color returned. Because of her years of experience, she was able to joke about it, but for those of you who have never witnessed breath holding, be cautious and don't assume it's nothing.

Above All Else — Safety First

If you have observed your child stop breathing and go unconscious, it is most important that you take him or her to a physician to rule out any medical concerns. Don't assume that you know what to do, especially if your child has passed out. Don't be afraid to call 911 in this situation because it is best to operate on the side of safety. Once you know that your child's health is medically sound, you can get back to the business of helping to change his or her behavior.

The Best Solution

With a clean bill of health from your doctor, you can go about the business of abolishing breath holding. It may always scare the life out of you, but the most effective way to abolish breath holding is to ignore it. When breath holding no longer gives attention to your child it has lost its usefulness.

Avoiding Injury

The last thing you need is for your child to pass out and injure himself or herself when hitting the floor. To avoid this, if you see your child intentionally holding his or her breath, lead your child to a safe place where there is carpet.

By no means should you attempt to talk your child out of the behavior. If you do, you will only be providing attention to this situation and be certain it will occur again and again.

Stay in the room with your child for his or her own safety, but keep your attention on something else. When the breath holding episode is over, don't talk about it or reprimand. Act like it never happened. Remember you don't want to inadvertently feed the attention monster. Instead look for opportunities to give praise for good behaviors, no matter how insignificant. And now for the good news, most children give up breath holding by age four.

Wild and Crazy In All the Wrong Places

Why is it that some children go bananas out in public? It is as if their bodies have been taken over by aliens and as a parent, you are mortified. Right in front of your eyes, your child becomes bratty, loud, and obstinate. With all those strangers peering at you and your wild kid, it's easy to feel intimidated, embarrassed, and totally inadequate. If you were at home, your reaction as a parent would be automatic. But out in the public eye you feel completely exposed. You freeze up or lose your temper.

Be Prepared

Anticipate where you are going and how long you will be there. If the day is going to be too long or too taxing, arrange for a baby-sitter.

I recently attended a wedding and sat behind a three year old in the church. The ceremony was beautiful but much too long for this toddler. As each minute passed, his behavior disintegrated a little more, a little more. His mother recognized that they were in a special place and tried to correct him with an icy stare. This only delighted the little boy. But his wise grandmother saw what was going on. She quietly took out a piece of paper and a pen for her grandson to scribble on. Problem solved.

If you are going someplace where your child is expected to sit quietly such as in a house of worship or a waiting room, bring along some favorite toys . . . or a surprise or two.

If you are out running errands, keep in mind how much your child can handle. Getting in and out of car seats and shopping carts gets exhausting after a while. Alone, you can cover lots of territory, but with a small child you may have to cut the shopping list in half. Include a surprise stop.

What To Do When It's Too Late

1. Hold Your Ground.

Tell your child what you expect of him or her and follow through.

We've all seen parents in the mall telling their child for the gazillionth time, "You better stop it! I'm not going to tell you again." Can you guess what their child hears? "Blah, blah, blah . . ."

Give your child a single warning and then follow through with a consequence.

"I asked you not to throw the ball in the store. And I told you that if you threw it again I would put the ball away. You've thrown the ball again. I am putting the ball away." End of discussion. No negotiations. No debates back and forth.

2. Time-Out.

It is possible to effectively use time-out in public places. Remove your child from the situation and take him or her to a quiet corner like a bathroom, dressing room, or even back to the car.

Explain clearly and simply what your child did wrong and why he or she is in time-out. Don't repeat yourself and go on and on. Tell your child what behavior you expect of him or her once your child pulls himself or herself together.

Once said, sit quietly with your child until he or she is ready to go back inside or to resume shopping. If your little one can't get it together, it's probably best to head for home. Under no circumstances should you ever leave a child alone in the car.

3. Losing A Privilege.

Sometimes losing a privilege can be an effective deterrent for a child. But most importantly, let the punishment fit the

---

Appropriate vz. Inappropriate Privilege Lozzez

Sometimes a parent can get so frustrated that they will conjure up extreme privilege losses just to make a point with their children. This plan often fails for two reasons:

1. The parent can't keep track of it because they're working or not home.

2. The child will see the situation as hopeless and not even try to improve.

Appropriate Privilege Loss:

Losing a privilege for an hour, day or week, i.e., no TV, computer, bicycle riding, dessert, telephone, allowance.

Inappropriate Privilege Loss:

Being grounded for months and months at a time.

Giving away your child's toys.

Forbidding them to speak to loved ones on the telephone.

Not allowing them to take part in something that clearly enhances their self-esteem, such as sports, the arts, music, or drama.

crime. Telling your daughter that you are going to give away her toys or your son that he can never ride his bike again is more hurtful than helpful.

Seek and Destroy

There's a good reason why grandmother puts the crystal away when Junior comes to visit. Children have a tendency to knock over and break things. Especially young children because their fine-motor skills are not fully developed. A two or three year old might reach for something and not yet have the coordination to grasp it properly. Bam! A treasured piggy bank hits the floor. Because children are naturally curious they might pull something apart to see how it works without realizing that they have no idea how to put it back together or that they have destroyed it. Children under two years have not put together the idea that there are some things you can throw down, like a stuffed animal, and then there are some things that you place down, like daddy's cellular phone. Still other children are active and impulsive and their hunger for discovery gets the better of them. That's why a child might keep winding and winding the toy until it jams. He just has to see what happens if he gives the key to the bird one last turn.

On the other hand, there are some children who will break or destroy something deliberately. Their reasons can be many, but for the most part, it is because they are angry about something and are having difficulty expressing it. Perhaps it's a new baby brother or a new school or because dad has a new lady friend. Perhaps it's because you went away for the weekend and left him with his grandmother.

What To Do

Many times children will stop being destructive simply because their parents have warned them. But if a gentle reminder or warning is not effective then you might consider these remedies:

1. Correct the Destructive or Potentially Dangerous Behavior and Role Play the Right Behavior.

Young children don't always know how to handle and touch things. For example, you see your child grabbing the dog's ears and realize that one or both are going to get hurt. Your child may not know that a dog's ears are tender and should be touched gently. Instead of waiting for the dog to teach this lesson to your child with a growl and a bite, intervene quickly. Explain why it's important to touch the dog gently and demonstrate how to correctly pet the dog. Then have your child give it a try. If your child has trouble grasping this idea, switch to a stuffed animal instead of the dog.

In my own life, I have one gigantic English Mastiff who weighs a mere 250 pounds and one adorable, curious little boy. Although I am an animal lover, I do realize that both animals and children can be unpredictable. I would recommend that you be vigilant in your supervision of both members of the family.

2. Teach How to Get Angry Feelings Across.

Sometimes children have difficulty getting their feelings across and as a result will act out. Learning how to express anger and frustration are two important lessons.

Labeling the Feelings. You don't have to act like a psychoanalyst to help your child label his or her feelings. It's much easier and more effective than you think. When you see your child slam down a toy, intervene and say, "Ah oh, you look frustrated. What's going on?" If your child is too young or can't verbalize the problem, intervene by redirecting him or her to another activity or by joining him or her for a while.

Learning Healthy Ways to Express Anger or Frustration. We all have different ways to let off steam. When it comes to children, they need some help to learn healthy ways to work out bad feelings. Some kids do well with physical activity — going outside to run around or maybe riding a bike for a while. Still others respond well to quiet time. With these children, putting on some soothing music and stretching out with a favorite stuffed animal or book can help them settle down. And there are others still who can release their feelings by drawing, coloring, or writing. You decide what works best for your little one.

3. Get Ahead of Destruction.

Limit the Number of Toys Your Child Plays with at a Given Time. Children can get overwhelmed when there are too many toys. They have a tendency to jump from one toy to the next and before you know it, their bedroom is a disaster and either something gets broken or they get hurt. Take out one toy at a time and then put the toy away. Your child is never too young to be part of the cleanup squad. When the blocks have lost their excitement gather them together and put them away.

Keep a Designated Play Area in the House. Pick an area in your house that is safe and far from the family heirlooms. Be sure that your children are playing in close proximity to where you are. It only takes a split second for an accident to occur.

Reward and Praise Your Child for Taking Care of His or Her Toys and for Cleaning Up. When your son is playing nicely with a toy, tell him. When your daughter cleans up after herself, praise her. Make cleaning up a room fun or a game. Young children love to be helpful and usually cannot resist a game. Who's going to clean up the fastest? Who's the best cleaner upper? Just tap into your imagination.

When All Else Fails . . . If your child continues to be destructive with a toy despite your interventions or warnings, then a time-out for the toy or your child may be called for. In either case, explain the reason for the time-out and how you expect your child to behave after out the time-out. Stick to your guns and avoid debates or discussions with your child.

But If Destructiveness Seems Malicious . . .   Children can experience intense feelings of anger, sorrow, loss, or betrayal and not know the appropriate ways to get those feelings across. Sometimes children will blame themselves for such things as their parents' divorce or the death of a family member even though they had nothing to do with it. In some cases, a child may play with matches, destroy things, hurt a younger child or small animal, or deliberately put themselves in danger. If your child's destructive behavior looks overly mean, revengeful, or thrill seeking to the point of danger and, despite your interventions, the behavior continues, consider seeking professional advice. (See Chapter 3, p. 57.)

When "No" Is A Foreign Word

"No" may be the first word a child learns and dislikes the most. As a child progresses from crawling to walking to climbing, a child may hear the "no" word several times a day or several times an hour. Children hate the "no" word.

Children as young as a year start to realize that "no" can be negotiated. Sometimes mom and dad sound like they really mean "no" but if I keep working on them they'll give in. Throw in a little whining and I'll cinch the deal.

Rule Number One: Say What You Mean and Mean What You Say

If you don't want your child to do something, then say so, and stick to your decision. It takes children a split second to realize when their parents are being wishy washy. If your child keeps getting up on the couch after you keep telling her not to, guess what? Your daughter has learned to not take you seriously. Why? Because you say "no" but don't follow through. If you want your child to listen to your correction, then issue a warning, then act.

Rule Number Two: Don't Sound Like A Broken Record

Remember that mom in the department store who keeps saying, "Don't touch that. Don't touch that. I *said* don't touch that. Did you hear me? I said don't touch that."

She has become a broken record and is no longer in control. This mom would be better off by first telling her child the behavior she expects, followed by a warning of what would happen if her wishes are not carried out. If her child does not listen then she must follow through on the consequence.

Rule Number Three: Don't Give In To Debates

If you feel strongly about saying "no" to your child for something then avoid being roped in for a debate. Explain once

---

Putting Some Oomph Behind Those "NO's"

+ **Tune Out.** If you have said no to your child, stick to that decision by tuning out any and all whining or pleas for mercy. Be prepared that your child could become quite dramatic, resort to begging, or even throw a tantrum. Nonetheless, tune out.

+ **Three Strikes.** Give your child three warnings before you hand down the consequence. After the third warning, briefly explain that he or she had three chances to not get into trouble. After that, stick to your word and give out the consequence. Remember, your child made a decision to not take your warnings seriously and made the choice to receive the consequence.

why you are saying no and indicate that the discussion is over. If your child persists, ignore him or her if possible.

Interrupting

"But mom, I want to ask you one thing. One thing. Mom, can I ask you one thing. Just one thing!"

All children, young or old, interrupt their parents. The telephone rings and there's your little one circling your legs with arms reaching up. One minute your child is completely absorbed with a coloring book or puzzle and then a friend comes over for coffee. Bing! Right by your side at the kitchen table. It's as if some kind of magnetic pull is keeping him or her stuck to the table.

Children interrupt their parents because they want their attention. Period. And if your child gets your attention whenever he or she interrupts, your child will do it again and again. Your child will learn that not only is it okay to interrupt *you,* but others as well.

When it comes to interrupting, children need to learn two things: First, how to wait to be heard; second, how to appropriately get someone's attention.

Waiting to be Heard

If your child is interrupting your conversation, acknowledge that you hear him or her and ask your child to be patient for a few moments. Try to get back to your child quickly so that your little one learns that you mean what you say and that if he or she waits, you will listen.

Good Manners

Start early to teach your child how to appropriately interact with others. Young toddlers can learn to say please, excuse me, and thank you if encouraged and praised often. Remember also

Your Time, My Time, and Our Time. What Time Is It Now?

This is a lovely, gentle intervention that I have stolen from a dear friend to share with you . . .

One night at a meeting, my friend had to bring her little girl along because she didn't have a baby-sitter. As she was leading the meeting, the little girl, who had been quietly playing in another room, started to interrupt her mother. In a quiet voice, my friend took her daughter's hand and said, "There's your time, my time, and our time. What time do you think it is now?" The little girl answered, "Your time." My friend then replied, "That's right, this is mommy's time. You go back to playing and I will see you later. Thanks honey. I love you" and placed a kiss on her head. The little girl went back to her game in the other room.

that little children watch their moms and dads to see just how to behave. You're teaching your child something every day whether it's answering a telephone, greeting a friend, or thanking a store clerk. Whenever I am on the telephone my two-year-old goes to his telephone and mimics my conversation and body language. Sometimes it's like looking in a mirror. Here I am chatting away with my hand on my hip and there he

is talking with his hand on his hip. It's amazing but children will mimic our facial and body gestures, verbal expressions, and reaction styles.

Please Stop Whining!!

Talk about a button pusher! Whining is the one sure way to push parents' buttons enough to have them lose their cool. Sometimes it has the same effect as fingernails across a blackboard. Make that child stop that whining now!

Whining has its roots in frustration. Maybe your child wants your attention and isn't getting it. Or perhaps your child has grown bored, tired, or hungry. And sometimes it's all these reasons combined. A child persists with a whiny voice until one of two things happens: either you give in to his or her demands or you lose your temper. Either way your child is getting a healthy dose of attention.

Whining is one of the ways your child is trying to communicate with you. Small children don't have the vocabulary or expressive skills to get all their feelings across. When children feel as if they are not being heard, they will change their voice to a whine. Whining persists because it works.

Whining usually starts at about two and a half and eases up by age four. However, like all behaviors, whining depends on the individual child. Some children never whine while others continue whining every day of their life.

What To Do

The best way to handle whining is to determine what caused it in the first place so as to avoid it in the future.

Physical Discomfort

First things first, determine if there is a physical reason for your child's whiny voice. Does your child need a diaper change? Is he or she hungry? Is your child's finger stuck in the VCR?

Boredom

Children can become bored anywhere if there isn't something to hold their attention. Even a visit to grandma's house can lose its appeal if there isn't enough to do. Bring a variety of things for your child to play with when traveling or visiting.

At home encourage your child to play independently by praising your child when he or she does.

Frustration and Toys

While toddlers like nothing better than to play, they can quickly become frustrated if a toy is beyond their mental or motor ability. When buying toys look for the suggested age on the side of the box. If a friend or relative gives your child a toy beyond his or her ability, put it away until the time is right.

Getting A Handle On Whining

Ask for a Normal Tone of Voice

When your child pleads with you in a whining voice, explain that you will only answer when he or she speaks normally.

Ignore a Whiney Voice

When your child persists in whining it is important to ignore it completely. You might say, "I want to help you because I can see you're upset, but I will only help you when you speak in your normal voice."

Don't Answer Your Child in a Whiney Voice

Even though you are reaching your limit, do not answer a whining child in a whining voice. Making fun of your child's whining will only increase the whining and perhaps cause him or her to conclude that it is acceptable behavior. Role model the behavior you want your child to imitate.

Don't Label Your Child as the "Whiner"

When a child hears himself labeled as a whiner, or anything else for that matter, it can become a self-fulfilling prophecy. "If I am called the 'whiner' then that must be who I am."

Time-Out

Give a quick time-out if your child persists in whining but first give him or her a warning. "I would like for you to speak to me in a normal voice. If you cannot then you will have a time-out." Then, when the whining continues, "I asked you to use a normal voice and you did not. You are going to time-out." The general rule of thumb is one minute for every year of the child. If a child is four years old they would have a four minute time-out. For more advice on time-out refer to the Sensible Solutions chapter.

Biting, Hitting, and Spitting

It doesn't take much for a group of preschoolers to begin biting, hitting, or spitting. Just ask any preschool teacher. These are immature behaviors frequently seen in young children who have not yet learned to appropriately express their feelings.

What To Do

Intervene Quickly

When you see your child involved in these types of behaviors, intervene immediately because someone could get hurt. State firmly what you will and will not allow. "I like that you are playing together but there is to be no biting. Everyone understand that?"

Supervise Children at Play

Horse play can lead to tears when children play together. Keep a close eye on how the children are playing so as to redirect when the behavior becomes wild.

Teach Your Child How To Get His or Her
Feelings Across

Children can become upset or frustrated quickly, particularly when they're not getting what they want. When you see the potential for trouble intervene by helping your child express him or herself.

Remove the Problem

If you see that the children cannot play with a toy without fighting over it, it may be best to remove it. But first give fair warning; "I want you kids to share that truck and take turns. If you can't, it will be put away."

Caught in the Act

Catching a child in the act of hurting another child is the best time to intervene. Waiting until later is nearly always ineffective because often you forget about it, something else gets in the way, or your child becomes confused about what he or she did wrong.

Time-Out

Intervene immediately with a time-out when you see hitting, biting, or spitting.

Don't Let Your Children Hit or Bite You

Sometimes very small children will hit or bite their parents as a way of communicating without realizing that it is harmful. For children under age two, explain gently but firmly that it is not okay to hit or bite. Demonstrate on them the behavior you want them to learn. "Don't bite mom. Make nice like this." Most young children are able to understand this fairly easily. Biting a child back doesn't help him or her learn any faster. It just hurts and teaches your child that if you can do it, your child can do it too.

Children over age two should understand that hitting, biting, and spitting are unacceptable. Stop everything when it occurs by saying, "You are not to bite me. Ever." If it happens again, stop the activity your child is involved with and use time-out. Even if you must leave where you are, it is important for your child to know that there are no exceptions to this rule.

Teach Your Child How to Apologize

Before taking your child to time-out have your child apologize to the person he or she hit, bit, or spat on. At the same time have your child say why it was wrong to do it. "I was wrong to bite you and I am sorry if I hurt you." When your child returns from a time-out don't remind or threaten him or her with "You better not do that again." Instead begin a fresh start by stating what you would like to see happen. "Welcome back Billy. Let's see everyone have a good time."

Bullies

When we think of a bully we usually picture the big kid on the playground knocking everybody down or the muscleman at the beach kicking sand in some little guy's face. Truth is bullies come in all shapes, sizes, and sexes. There are many ways a bully can be tough without being physical. A bully can be the smallest child on the block who has the ability to verbally or mentally intimidate the rest of the children into doing whatever he or she wants. The other truth is that no one likes a bully. They not only hurt other people but themselves as well. If you've noticed your child acting like a bully it's smart to do something about it before he or she has alienated him or herself from every child on the block and at school.

Although it would be easy to conclude that a bully is simply mean, it is not really the truth. A bully is an insecure child. The aggressive behavior is often a mask used to hide and overcompensate for those insecure feelings. Bullies often find themselves in a no-win situation. Their aggressive nature chases children away and as the children move away the insecure feelings increase.

When Your Child Is The Bully

Work on Self-Esteem

Take a look at the things your child does well and praise him or her for them. A child doesn't have to be athletic or a straight-A student to be praised. Children love praise from their moms and dads for the small things, like taking a cup to the sink or sitting still for 15 minutes.

Offer Responsibility

Although we have a tendency to think that punishment is the best medicine for a bully, there may be better options. One way to stop the insecurity monster from being fed is to ask your child to do something that he or she perceives as a privilege and that requires responsibility. Perhaps it's something as simple as walking the dog, playing the messages on the answering machine, or paying the person who delivers the newspaper.

Role Play

Take time with your child to discuss situations in which he or she is likely to act like a bully. Have your child be the child who is picked on while you play the bully. This is not really a "so how to do you like it kid" technique as much as a way for your child to understand the feelings of other people and to learn new ways to express feelings and thoughts. The role play might conclude with a situation in which your child plays the bully who decides to behave differently.

Don't You Be Bullied

It may sound silly but a child can also bully an adult. Avoiding conflicts so as not to "rock the boat" won't help your child to learn how to settle his or her differences. Stand firm and be consistent with your child.

When Things Get Broken or Destroyed

If your child has been involved in a situation where something gets broken, he or she should be held responsible for doing something about it. For example, if your child breaks a friend's bicycle, he or she might do extra jobs around the house, earning money to pay for the damage.

When It's Your Child Who Is Being Bullied

Ignore the Bully

What bullies seem to like best of all is to be intimidating or to cause someone to cry, especially in front of other peers. Your child might try to keep his or her composure and to tune out the bully. But warn your child that the bully will get worse before he or she decides to give up and move on to the next child.

When Ignoring Is Impossible

Sometimes no matter how hard you try to ignore a bully, he or she won't go away. It's time to become assertive. Show your child how to stand confidently and look the bully directly in the eye while saying, "Stop calling me names. I don't like it," or " This is getting boring. Everyday it's the same old thing. You should get a life." Often statements like these will defuse the situation and the bully will move on. However the notion of standing eyeball to eyeball with a bully can be very frightening. Role play the situation in a variety of ways until your child feels confident.

Using Humor

Most bullies like to see the intimidation and fear on their victim's face. It gives them power and makes them feel in control. The last thing a bully expects from their victim is a sense of humor. Your child could say something like, "You know . . . you're never around when I need you. Where have you been? I could have used you in gym this morning. Do me a favor and don't disappear on me."

Have Your Child Ask the Bully For Help or Advice

Sometimes solutions are found in the least obvious places. Bullies rarely expect anyone to ask for their opinion or help on anything.

A Child-Teacher Meeting

If your child's bully is at school, consider having your child request a teacher's conference. "Mrs. Anderson, I would like to have a teacher's conference with you. I would like to have Naomi there too because I'm having a problem with her." This intervention can work very effectively with children as young as four.

Calling the Parents

If the bullying continues in spite of your child's attempts to stop it, calling the bully's parents may be your best bet. Sometimes parents have no idea that their child is bullying other children and will intervene immediately. Beware, however, some parents will have that, "Not my Johnny" attitude. If that's the case, you may have to talk with your child and advise him or her to keep away from that child.

Encourage Your Child To Buddy-Up

Bullies usually look to single out the kid who stays to himself or herself and is less likely to go after a group of children.

A Last Thought

Parents Should Try Not To Interfere With Their Child's Squabbles

Settling disputes and conflict is one of the important lessons a child needs to learn on the road to adulthood. Untangling a disagreement is uncomfortable (for most of us, anyway) and one we all would like to avoid. For those reasons, it is important for your children to learn how to amicably settle their differences. And besides, how many times have you seen your children in a fight with other kids on your block only to have it all forgotten 10 minutes later?

When it comes to a bully, use your intuition to decide if your child can manage this problem without you or if it is too big for him or her to handle alone. Always operate on the side of safety and intervene immediately if you fear that your child could get harmed in any way.

Sometimes a child can't or won't express to his or her parents that another child is bothering him or her. Little children often think that they are being picked upon because of something that they must be doing wrong. Older children might not talk about a bully for fear of looking stupid or weak. It's always best to keep an eye on the children your child plays with. If your child seems uncomfortable around a child or is reluctant to go over to his or her house when invited, check it out.

Chapter 6

Ask the
Tantrum Doctor

Q: *My husband and I are having marital problems and decided to separate for a while. He has moved out and takes our three children on weekends. This year has been difficult on everybody because on top of our marital problems, we've lost our dog and my husband's father was diagnosed with cancer. Two of our children don't seem too concerned about what is going on, but our youngest, who is six, is giving us a terrible time. Even though we always called her our "sensitive" one, her behavior has become a real challenge. She screams when things don't go her way and throws herself on the ground whenever I go to leave the house. She can throw some world-class tantrums. She has gotten very clingy with me, following me through the house and constantly begging to sleep in my bed. We've been called to the school a few times to talk with the teacher who says our daughter can't settle down or finish her work. Now the teacher is saying that she may have Attention Deficit Disorder. Is she going back to the terrible two's, should I have her tested, or what? I'm at a loss here.*

A: Your family has certainly been going through some trying
times. You've not only experienced a crisis in your marriage, but the loss of a loved family pet and concern for
your father-in-law's health. Separation and divorce are
difficult for anyone but these events are especially hard on
children. Many children experience their parent's break-
up as a true trauma. Children not only experience fear that
family members will disappear but also grieve for the loss
of the family life they once knew. Your situation has been
exacerbated by other circumstances as well.

It is not unusual for children to become possessive of
a parent during a traumatic period. They are frightened
and seek both your comfort as well as your protection.
Your daughter's clinging and tantrums when you try to go
are really her attempt to say, "I'm afraid if you leave you
won't come back."

Your daughter needs a lot of reassurance at this time.
Her immature behaviors and explosive tantrums are tem-
porary. If she needs a little more attention or comforting
then it is best to give them to her. Talk with her about what
she's feeling and try to answer her questions.

It is not surprising that your daughter's stress is revealing
itself at school. She may be having a difficult time settling
down to work because she feels unsettled inside. Unless you
had valid concerns about Attention Deficit Disorder prior to
your marital problems, I would leave that alone for the
moment and focus on the present concerns. Alert your
daughter's teacher to what is happening in your home. Keep
a steady and consistent schedule with your daughter to help
her feel more secure. As an extra measure of assurance you
might pop little notes in her lunch box or a funny photograph in her school books. This will give your daughter a
sense of security and love when she is away from you.

As for your recent separation, be honest with all your children about what is really going on. Children are often a lot more aware of the reality of a situation then we adults give them credit. Children also have a way of blaming themselves for their parents' problems. Explain that their dad is living someplace else because of a concern between both of you and not because of them. Reassure them that no matter what happens they will always have their mom and dad who love them very much.

Q: *The other day while my sister was at the house, my four-year-old son threw a tantrum. Normally I see them coming before they hit but I was so busy talking that I missed all the clues. Although my son doesn't have tantrums all the time, like all toddlers he does have them. And I think that I handle my son's tantrums the right way. Anyhow he let out a scream and threw himself on the ground. At first I was frightened because he smacked his head so hard on the tile. After checking his head I gently picked him up and laid him down on his bedroom carpet. In a quiet voice I said, "I can see that you are very upset. I really hope you feel better. When you are, I'll be right outside." With that I left his bedroom and went back to my sister. My sister was shaking her head and told me that I need to come down harder on my son or else he'll grow up spoiled. She said real time-out is when a child sits in a chair facing a wall. I told her that my style of time-out works for me and my son. My sister said I was only fooling myself. As for my son, he laid on the floor sobbing for about 20 minutes and then fell asleep. When he came out of the bedroom he was happy and went back to playing. I say problem solved. My sister says I'm afraid to be tough. What do you say?*

A: I applaud you for following your own instincts. No two children are the same, therefore no two children can be disciplined in the same way. The first step to being an effective parent is listening to your intuition about what you think works best for your own child. You took your son to a safe and quiet spot in the house and left him alone till the tantrum blew over. At the same time you didn't create space for a battle of wills over who was in charge. Your firm yet gentle manner let your son understand that he had something to work out and you would be there when he was calm. Unfortunately some parents don't allow the punishment to fit the crime and go way overboard. If what you do works then you have found a sensible and effective way to discipline your son.

Q: *I think I already have an out-of-control baby. My 18-month old son is having tantrums. I spoke to my pediatrician about the problem and she said that I should use time-out. I put my son in this time-out chair but he won't stay there. He jumps off and gets more hysterical. I tried to set an oven timer for five minutes but the problem got worse in just seconds. I even tried to hold him down on the chair while I explained that he had to stop acting this way. Forget it. We both were exhausted and I nearly lost my temper. Obviously I'm missing the boat on something. Help!*

A: The rule of thumb for using time-out is one minute for every year of the child. A four year old would therefore be timed-out four minutes. Unfortunately this doesn't always work, especially for very young children. Asking them to remain in one place for 30 seconds when they are upset is impossible, resulting in the problem you describe. It becomes a game of wills in which no one is the winner. The problem that originally sent your son to the time-out chair is forgotten and replaced with a new problem.

The key to this tangled little mess is that you react assertively to let your child know that he cannot continue misbehaving. Whether your child sits on a chair or lays on the floor is not important. In addition, it doesn't matter how long he stays there as long as he knows you are in charge.

The next time your son misbehaves try something different. Suppose he throws his toy truck across the room: First, tell him in a firm voice that throwing toys is not allowed. If he listens, praise him with a hug. Second, if your son throws the truck again, say, "Throwing toys is not okay. It's dangerous. I'm taking you to time-out." Third, take your son to a quiet room and sit him in a chair or gently lay him down on the floor. Say to him in a firm but quiet voice, "I want you to stay there until I tell you to get up." Wait about five seconds and say, "Now you can get up." The message to your child is that you are in charge and that he is cooperating with you. It eliminates the power struggle over whether or not he sits in a chair and for how long. The next time you use time-out wait a few more seconds before you give permission for your son to get up. Before long your son will be waiting for your signal before he gets up.

Q: *I had the most horrible scene with my three-year old daughter last week and am very ashamed of what happened. Every morning it's the same routine with her. I ask her to get dressed for day care and she says she won't. When I try to dress her she fights me and takes her clothes off. Frequently I'm late for work and rattled for the rest of the day. Last week I finally lost it. After 30 minutes of*

*begging her to get dressed, I dragged her out to the car as
she was — naked. We were both hysterical and crying.
Finally, feeling like a monster, I brought her inside and
called my husband to come home from work. When he
arrived home my daughter was still crying, still naked, and
lying on the kitchen floor. When my daughter saw her daddy
she stopped crying and got dressed. I was ready to be
committed. If this happens to me again, what should I do?*

A: There's no question that children can test both our patience and our sanity. A stubborn toddler could shake up
even the toughest drill sergeant if that toddler sets her
mind to it. It sounds as if it was a difficult morning for
everyone. You did the right thing by calling your husband
before you really lost control of your temper.

The first thing to consider is there a problem at your
daughter's day care center? Operate on the side of safety
to ensure that she is comfortable and secure when in the
hands of others. With this safety issue out of the way, it's
likely that the problem lies in the fact that she is three
years old and can't quite follow the morning routine. A
toddler's concept of time is different than an adult's. Adults
monitor their activities by reading a clock. Most toddlers
can't tell time and have not yet developed an understanding of being prompt or running late. They monitor themselves through activities, for example, play time comes
after lunch.

To keep your morning schedule on track, start by getting ready the night before. Help your daughter pick out
her clothes and get everything ready for the next day. This
would include fixing her lunch and deciding what she
would like to take in her backpack. The key is in doing this
with your daughter so she feels involved in and motivated
for the next day at day care. While you and your daughter
are making these preparations, talk about the types of

things she likes to do and what she is looking forward to doing tomorrow. The next morning talk up the fun she is going to have. If your daughter still dawdles while getting dressed, have her bring her clothes into your room so that you can get dressed together. Two ladies getting dressed for work. Maybe you could give her a little spritz of your perfume.

When your daughter is not looking, put a little note or photo in her lunch box. Although she can't yet read, your daughter may be delighted to find a heart or a happy face from her mommy. We take so many photographs of our children, throw in one that will give her a chuckle. The underlying message to your daughter is, "I'm with you and I love you."

You might also consider breaking up the family's morning routine by having your husband take your daughter to day care from time to time. Maybe they could have a special morning where they go out for a quick breakfast en route to day care. This frees you up to have a morning to yourself once in a while.

Q: *I now dread going food shopping with my three-and-a-half year old son. He always wants something he can't have and then there's an explosion. He screams and acts likes a nut. Everybody's watching and I know what they're saying, "What a brat. Nice mother. Can't you control him?" I try talking to him and threatening that I'm going to bring him home to bed but nothing works. Last week was the all-time worst. He wasn't getting his way and he bit me right on my breast. It hurt so much that I saw stars. Fighting back my own tears, I ignored him the rest of the time. Needless to say my son never stopped carrying on until we got home. Later that day my husband scolded him but even that seemed useless. My breast is*

*actually bruised. Is there something wrong with my son or
am I a terrible mother?*

A: Easy with the guilt. You were injured once, no need to be
injured twice. Food shopping with a toddler can bring on
a host of challenges. They get bored, or they see something that they must have. We all dread public tantrums
because everybody stares and we feel so stupid. But believe me, there isn't an adult watching who hasn't been in
your place at least once.

First, be selective about the time of day when you
choose to go shopping with your little one. Is it too close
to a nap or dinner time? Pick a time when he's rested and
not hungry. Second, like a boy scout, be prepared. Bring
along a goodie bag that contains a favorite snack, small
toy, and a surprise. Third, have your son be your assistant
by holding the food list or helping you look for items. I am
not, however, suggesting that you set him loose in the
store or get out of your sight for a single minute. What I
am suggesting is that he sit in the cart and be the look-out
for different items when you get to that aisle. Finally, keep
your shopping excursions short. By planning ahead and
making shopping fun you increase the likelihood that you'll
both have a pleasant experience.

Now let's address this biting issue. Your son must learn
that it is not okay to bite anyone. Biting, hitting, or harm-
ing calls for an immediate reaction from a parent. When
you ignore being injured by your son, you inadvertently
give the message that he holds authority over you. If the
situation happens again, stop what you are doing and say
to your son in a calm but firm voice, "It is never okay to
bite me or anyone. We are now going home and you will
spend the rest of the day inside. There will be no TV and
you will go to bed early." Follow through and leave the

store even if your grocery cart is full. Do not negotiate a second chance or get into any debates.

Q: *I am very concerned about my seven-year-old daughter who is having what I consider very serious tantrums. My daughter's tantrums are so severe that she throws furniture and screams for up to an hour. There seems to be no way to stop her once she gets going. I'm afraid that she could hurt herself or one of us. She does have a younger sister, but she seems to adore her so I don't think it's a case of sibling jealously. I must tell you also that I work full-time and travel quite a bit. My husband takes care of the girls and never has this problem with my daughter. I'm starting to think she hates me. Do we both need therapy? And isn't she too old to be having tantrums?*

A: Despite what you may find in the literature, tantrums know no age limit. True, most children grow out of the tantrum stage by age five or six but others may continue with this problem all through their development. When children don't have an appropriate channel to release their anger or frustration, they explode.

You have provided some interesting clues to this dilemma. The tantrums occur with you and not your husband. Your work takes you out of the home quite often. Your daughter may be trying to say that she needs you but doesn't have the right means to communicate those feelings.

First, observe your daughter closely to notice when her mood is changing and a possible tantrum may be coming. Often an older child will give clues that they are feeling angry or needy. Listen to her voice and watch her body language. Knowing what's brewing gives you the opportunity to intervene before it is too late. You might approach her with a hug and say, "Hey kiddo, what's up?"

Maybe you both could curl up on a couch and talk about it for a while. If you have started dinner, ask her to help. You could even wear matching aprons and have some fun with it.

Second, your daughter may be having trouble adjusting to your work schedule. Overnight business trips are often disruptive to a child's routine. In addition, your daughter may simply miss you. I know of a sweet intervention that can be very effective in this situation. Talk to your daughter about how much you miss her when you are on the road. Tell her that you have thought of a way to be together even when apart. Go to the store with your daughter and purchase something that you both can wear. For example, buy two of the same night shirt. Explain that when you both wear the night shirts you'll know that you are thinking of each other. You might buy two of the same costume necklace or bracelet and tell her that whenever she looks at it, she will know that you love her and are thinking about her. Even when you are apart, you can be together. This may be all the reassurance your daughter needs when you are on the road.

Third, look for any and all opportunities to catch your daughter behaving well. Catch her off guard with a hug and a kiss. Be playful with her. This suggestion and the ones above give you as a parent the chance to lessen the likelihood of a tantrum. You are giving her attention, listening to her concerns, and reassuring her that you are together even when apart.

The tantrums you described sound nasty and potentially dangerous. While you are doing my other suggestions, it is important to know how to intervene when a serious tantrum appears. When children start to throw furniture, they are out of control. Ignoring a child in this situation is not wise. Trying to talk your daughter out of the tantrum will probably only exacerbate the problem. It may be necessary to physically restrain her until the tantrum subsides. Being careful not to hurt yourself or her, attempt to gently lie her on the floor, preferably one with carpeting. Without speaking hold her legs and arms down firmly. Your daughter is likely to resist this restraint so hold on tightly. If she is kicking her legs, roll her over onto her stomach, cross her legs at the ankle and hold them down. The idea is restrain your daughter in a safe manner to avoid injury. Hold her quietly until she has stopped crying and is breathing quietly.

Q: *I have a 19-month-old-son who is cared for by a nanny while I am working. I do have the good fortune of working from my home so I can hear and see them all day long. So far it has worked out great. My son loves the woman who cares for him. They play together and have a really great time. The problem is that at 5:00 when the nanny says good-bye, my son becomes very whiney and cranky. I'm trying to fix dinner, feed the dogs, and keep him smiling all at the same time. He's constantly pulling on my pants or asking to be carried. He's a really great little guy but I'm starting to worry that he is spoiled.*

A: The hours just before dinner can be difficult for a toddler. Even though they are starting to run down their batteries they want to keep going and going. In addition, toddlers sometimes have trouble transitioning from one person or one thing to another. He has spent the day with one person and now is with someone else (even if it is Mom). Toddlers can be resistant to a change of activity.

When the nanny leaves at 5:00, take your son to a quiet spot in the house and play for a little while. You might want to put on some peaceful music to create a more relaxing atmosphere. Reconnect with your son by talking about how his day went. After a little while, tell him that it's time to make supper and feed the dogs. Ask him to be your assistant. Allow him to carry the dog dishes and scoop the food. Talk to him about what you both will do next, "OK, we fed the dogs, now it's time to get our dinners ready." Allow him to help you as much as possible. He can carry the placemats and napkins to the table or get his place ready. While you're waiting for everything to cook, spend some quiet time with your son. If you can't because of time constraints or you have other children, then set your son up with an activity while you are finishing.

Q: *My husband and I are about to take our first airplane trip with our daughter. She is 14 months old and has never been on an airplane before. I've heard and seen all the horror stories about traveling with a baby. I don't want to be the family on the plane that nobody wants to sit next to. I want to plan ahead and be prepared. Do you have any suggestions?*

A: Ah yes, the dreaded airplane trip. Deciding to be prepared can make the difference between a pleasant experience and a nightmare. For several reasons I would suggest you purchase a seat for your daughter rather than sitting her on your lap for the flight. Seating on airplanes is cramped as it is without a baby sitting on you for several hours. If the plane gets warm, then you will both be uncomfortable and irritable. Asking a young child to sit happily on someone's lap for several hours is a lesson in frustration. But more importantly than all of that, it is much safer for your daughter to be in her own individual seat. Think about it — everyone on the plane is secured into a seat in case of turbulence or an emergency except your child. Bring along your daughter's car seat for extra safety. The added expense could put a crimp in the vacation budget but it could also save her life.

Parents who prepare for travel with a child stand a better chance of having a pleasant trip. Book early and request the bulkhead seats up front instead of the back rows. You'll have a shorter distance to trudge all your paraphernalia through the plane. The bulkhead seats will give you more leg room and easier access to your child. Your travel agent should be able to provide you with boarding passes so that you can avoid long lines at the gate. Try to reserve a flight at times when your daughter would normally be sleeping, such as nap or bedtime.

Bring along your child's favorite foods. Relying upon the meal served by the airline could be a disaster if your daughter won't touch it. Include finger foods like blueberries, raisons, and unsalted pretzels. Planes are notoriously dry so don't forget the extra juice or a bottle of water. Bring small toys that fit in a baby bag but that are appropriate for a 14 month old. Leave the toys that beep and bark at home. Everyone on the plane will be infinitely grateful. Make sure to bring a few surprises for your child to open and discover, such as small toys that she has never seen before. Children at this age love small books with little finger puppets or pop-up pictures. If you have a pocket calculator, bring it along. Your daughter may love pushing the buttons and watching the numbers appear. The temperature inside a plane is always unpredictable so bring along a sweater or a small baby blanket.

Did you ever notice how all the "screaming babies" howl during takeoff and landing? Flying can be tough on a small child's ears because of the changes in cabin pressure. Have your daughter drink from a bottle or sippy-cup as the plane is moving down the runway or coming in for a landing. The sucking and swallowing helps to relieve the pressure that builds up in the ears. If your daughter gets very uncomfortable ask the stewardess for two hot towels. After making sure that they are not too hot, place a towel over each ear. The heat from the towels will expand the middle ear and relieve pressure on the eardrum. Have a good flight!

Chapter 7
Relax Baby

A child's life seems so simple and uncomplicated. There's lots of time to play, no bills to pay, and no responsibilities to worry about. But is this really so? Do children really live stress-free lives? Are children really immune to life's stressors that wear so many adults down to a nub?

According to statistics, children can and do experience stress in their lives. Children today are confronted, more than ever before, with such serious issues as

- Divorce
- Domestic violence
- Community crime
- School violence
- Media violence
- Drug and alcohol abuse

It's not uncommon for some moms and dads to think that their children are immune to stress in their home. In fact, there have been several circumstances when parents brought their children to my office with concerns of Attention Deficit Disorder or learning disabilities, when in fact, there was a crisis in the family.

I recall an afternoon when a mom brought her 10-year-old son in for an evaluation because she thought he might have a learning disability. Her son's grades were poor, he had few friends, and in-school testing suggested he could be mildly retarded. The school also expressed concern that this boy was obsessed with ambulances and suggested that he be treated by a psychiatrist.

As Mrs. Harney shared her thoughts with me she seemed nervous and very wound-up. She was a kind lady and cried as she described the problems Max was having in school. Max, meanwhile, sat quietly beside his mom, putting his arm around her as she spoke. He struck me as rather mature and sensitive for a 10 year old, and not at all like the boy described by the school in their reports.

I sensed that there was something else going on but that both mother and son shared a strong vow of secrecy. I asked Max to step out of the room so that I could speak privately for a few moments with mom. Once alone, I asked Mrs. Harney what else was going on in their lives. What was she neglecting to tell me? Mrs. Harney denied any trouble until I asked this question, "Tell me about your relationship with your husband." From the startled look on her face, I knew I had pressed a sensitive button.

Slowly, Mrs. Harney unfolded a home life filled with domestic violence. Her husband, Mr. Harney, had imprisoned his family within a reign of terror. He tapped the telephone, secretly videotaped them and had violently assaulted his wife in front of the children. Ten year old Max lived each day concerned not with the typical interests of other kids, but with the fear that his father would one day kill his mother. That's why he was so obsessed with ambulances. With this enormous secret out in the open, we were able to get down to the real issues: informing mom of the options available to her and how to get this family to a safe place.

Prescription for an OverTired Child

Start with a warm bubble bath . . .

Followed by a bottle or glass of warm milk . . .

Add soft, peaceful music . . .

Dim the lights . . .

Lay down for a snooze.

Fortunately, most children don't ever experience this level of stress in their lives. But children can experience mild to moderate levels of stress on a daily basis that may cause changes to their behavior, eating and sleeping habits, and performance at school.

As adults, we can look back on our childhoods as relatively carefree. Maybe we walked alone to school, had a snack after school, and then played outside or rode our bikes until our moms called us in for dinner. A few of us went off to pre-school, but the majority didn't begin school until kindergarten. Perhaps some of the boys played on Little League teams while the girls were Brownies or Blue Birds. Life was simpler and less hurried.

Today's child is more sophisticated than ever before and a lot busier. A large number enter day care as infants because both parents work or they are from single-parent households. It is generally expected that toddlers will begin preschool at age two or three. Outside of school, today's boys and girls play more team sports, in addition to music, computer, or drama lessons. Academically, many children are learning their basic concepts in preschool and may even be readers by the time they reach kindergarten. Some children are computer literate by age four.

Today's children come from different family environments than we knew. Twice as many children live in single-parent homes as in the 1970s. Approximately 50% have divorced parents. Weekends and holidays have to be coordinated between two homes. Often there is the adjustment to step-siblings when mom or dad remarry partners who have children from a previous marriage.

Today's children are being exposed to increasing amounts of violence in the media. Consider this: by age 18, the average young person will have viewed an estimated 200,000 acts of violence on television alone. Children's programming on Saturday mornings contain between 20 to 25 violent acts per hour.

With all that can confront our children, how can we help them to relax and calm down from life's daily stressors? Before we discuss specific ways to relieve stress, we might want to ask ourselves this burning questions: How stressful are the lives we lead? Have we become like hamsters on a treadmill, unable to get off and ultimately burning out? If you are wondering whether or not you could be one of those treadmill hamsters, ask yourselves the following questions:

Do You Have Hamster-On-A-Treadmill Syndrome?

- When you feel that your schedule is too busy, what's the first thing you cut out? Your free time or more work?
- How often do you really use that exercise equipment?
- Do you get your haircut or colored four or five weeks later than you really wanted to?
- Is your "One Day I'm Going To . . ." list getting taller than you?

I pose these questions to you for one important reason: If you lead an overcommitted busy life, chances are that your children do too. As role models, it is our job to teach our children how to achieve and how to wind down and replenish our energy levels.

The Power of Music

Enough cannot be said about the influence of music in our daily lives. We find music interwoven through every aspect of what we consider important. It's in our cars, televisions, places of worship, celebrations, and team sports. Music is part of our rituals that we hold near and dear. Imagine Christmas without "Jingle Bells." When you go to a wedding, what do you care about most? Be truthful, it's the food and the music. What's a birthday party without a chorus of Happy Birthday or the World Series without our national anthem?

While music can energize and get us up dancing, it can also be soothing and relaxing. Did you think that the music in your dentist's office was there by accident?

Whether you want to calm yourself, your child, or your family, music is a lovely way to start. Soft music in a home brings the tempo down. Infants and children find light instrumentals or lullabies soothing during nap and bedtime. Listening to music or singing songs with your children is a great way to spend time together.

Researchers have found that there is a connection between music and learning. Infants and toddlers benefit from music because it enhances their ability to process information. Music stimulates language development by encouraging listening and expressive language skills.

Music Resource Guide for You and Your Children

- *Music and Your Child's Education.* Consumer Information Catalog, Consumer Information Center, PO Box 100, Pueblo, CO 81002
- *Nurtured by Love.* By S. Suzuki. Norris, TN: Exposition Press, 1969, 121 pages.

- *Sound Health: The Music and Sounds that Make Us Whole.* By Steven Halpern and Savory Louis. New York: Harper, 1985, 192 pages.
- *Alcazar's Catalog of Children's Music.* PO Box 429, Waterbury, VT 05676. Phone: 1 (800) 541-9904.
- *Anyone Can Whistle.* PO Box 4407, Kingston, NY 12401. Phone: 1 (800) 435-8863.
- *Music for Little People.* Box 1460, Redway, CA 95560. Phone: 1 (800) 727-2233.
- *Music in Music.* PO Box 833814, Richardson, TX 75083-3814. Phone: 1 (800) 445-0649.
- *NEMC'S Band and Orchestra Instrument Catalog.* National Educational Music Company, Ltd., 1181 Route 22, Box 1130, Mountainside, NJ 07092. Phone: 1 (800) 526-4593.

Audiocassette:

- *The Classical Child (series).* For children from birth to seven years. Available through: Hand in Hand, Catalogue Center, Route 26, RR 1, Box 1425, Oxford, ME 04270-9711. Phone: 1 (800) 872-9745.
- *Mr. Bach Comes to Call.* For children ages six and over. Available through: The Children's Group, Music for Little People, Box 1460, Redway, CA 95560. Phone: 1 (800) 727-2233.
- *Lullaby Magic.* For children from birth to seven years. By Joanne Bartels. Discovery Music, 5554 Calhoun Avenue, Van Nuys, CA 91401. Phone: 1 (800) 451-5175.
- *Lullaby Berceuse.* For children from birth to seven years. Oak Street Music, 93 Lombard Avenue, Suite 108, Winnepeg, Manitoba, Canada R3B, 3B1. Phone: (204) 957-0085.
- *Rock-A-Bye Baby.* For children four years and under. Purple Balloon Players, GAA Corp., 206 Adamson Industrial Blvd., Carrollton, GA 30117.

- *Rock-A-Bye Collection.* For children four years and under. Someday Baby, Inc., 1508 16th Avenue South, Nashville, TE 37212.
- *Peter and the Wolf.* For children from one and over. Aristoplay, PO Box 7529, Ann Arbor, MI 48107. Phone: 1 (800) 634-7738.
- *A Child's Celebration of Show Tunes.* For children of all ages. Music for Little People, Box 1460, Redway, CA 95560. Phone: 1 (800) 727-2233.
- *Star Dreamer: Nightsongs and Lullabies.* For children under six. By Priscilla Herdman. Alcazar's Catalog of Children's Music, PO Box 429, Waterbury, VT 05676. Phone: 1 (800) 541-9904.
- *G'night Wolfgang.* For children under six. By Ric Louchard. Music for Little People, PO Box 1460, Redway, CA 95560. Phone: 1 (800) 727-2233.

Video Collection:

- *This Pretty Planet: Tom Chapin Live in Concert.* For children of all ages. Sony Kids Video, 1700 Broadway, NY, NY 10019. Phone: (212) 689-8897.
- *Baby's Bedtime and Baby's Morningtime.* For children ages two to five. Music by Judy Collins. Lightyear Entertainment, Empire State Building, 350 Fifth Avenue, Suite 5101, NY, NY 10118. Phone: (212) 563-4610.
- *Raffi in Concert.* For ages two and up. A & M Video, 1416 North Labrea Avenue, Hollywood, CA 90028. Phone: (213) 469-2411.

Relax, Don't Hurry

With overburdened schedules and nonstop commitments, a little quiet can go a long, long way. Quiet time affords you the

pleasure of being with your child and strengthening the bonds that hold you together. Here are just a few ideas to get you started.

Reading Together

Make reading a part of your daily ritual with your children. Not only is it a good way to settle down after a busy day, but it lays the foundation for language development and reading skills. Children who are read to as infants and toddlers are more likely to be readers as adults. Besides, children love to be read to because they can cuddle up close with mom or dad. Don't be surprised if your little one asks for the same story over and over. Toddlers learn through repetition of sounds in language. Stories will develop greater meaning for them as they are read again and again.

Some Favorite Books for Children

- *Hope For The Flowers* (1972). Trina Paulus, New York: A Newman Book/Paulist Press. For ages five and up.
- *Charlotte's Web* (1952). E.B. White. New York: HarperCollins. For ages five and up. For children of all ages.
- *The House at Pooh Corner* (1928). A.A. Milne. For ages five and up.
- *The Children's Book of Virtues* (1995). William J. Bennett. New York: Simon and Schuster. For children of all ages.
- *The Velveteen Rabbit* (1983). Margery Williams. New York: Henry Holt and Company. For children of all ages.

- *Time for Bed* (1993). Mem Fox. New York: Harcourt Brace. For infants and children up to three.
- *Where the Wild Things Are* (1963). Maurice Sendak. New York: HarperCollins. For children of all ages.
- *Through Moon and Stars and Night Skies* (1990). Ann Turner. New York: HarperCollins. For ages three and up.
- *The Pop-up Mice of Mr. Brice* (1989). Theo LeSieg. New York: Random House. For ages two to six.
- *The Cat in the Hat* (1957). Dr. Seuss. New York: Random House. For children of all ages.
- *The Very Hungry Caterpillar* (1987). Eric Caile. New York: Putnam and Grosset. For infants and children up to age four.
- *The Tenth Good Thing About Barney* (1971). Judith Viorst. New York: Macmillan. For ages four and up.
- *We Are All Alike . . . We Are All Different* (1991). Cheltenham Elementary School Kindergartners. New York: Scholastic. For ages three and up.
- *A Light in the Attic* (1981). Shel Silverstein. New York: HarperCollins. For children of all ages.
- *Happy Birthday Moon* (1982). Frank Asch. New York: Simon and Schuster. For ages two and up.

Quiet Activities

There are many quiet activities you can do with your child either in your home or outside. A quiet activity is something which offers you some enjoyment, relaxation, and fun. For some that means curling up together with a good book while for others that means planting a garden or building a bird cage. Your interests are unique to you and your children. The thing to remember is that it is important for us all to break from the rigors of our daily lives and spend time simply enjoying each other's company.

My dad used to say that the best things in life are free. There are many things a family can do outside that are free or just about. Here's just a few ideas to get you thinking:

- Walking along a beach, lake, or through a park
- Feeding the ducks with some bread from home
- Going to a free concert in your community
- Studying the stars from your backyard
- Watching airplanes land at the airport

There are other activities you can do with your children right inside your home. Yes, there's always the option of just watching television. Many of us do plenty of that every night. But the trouble with only watching television is that no one speaks to each other. With children growing up so fast these days, wouldn't it be better to sometimes engage them in activities that require some communication, thinking, and cooperation? Whether you have cabin fever during a cold winter, a rainy day, or you just feel like staying in, these activities might be fun:

- Puzzles and board games
- Chess
- Coloring and drawing
- Cooking and baking
- Playing cards
- Planting a vegetable or flower garden
- Crafts of all kinds . . . sewing, woodwork
- Playing dress up
- Learning a foreign language or musical instrument together
- Trace your family tree

Hugs, Hugs, and More Hugs

It sounds simplistic and may be easily overlooked but hug your children every day and for no reason at all. In our gentle

---

Quiet Activity Idea

You probably have boxes and boxes of photographs that you've been planning to put into photo albums for years. How about spending a quiet afternoon putting them in albums with your children? Not only is it a nice way to be together but it gives your children a sense of family history.

---

touch, we assure our children that not only do we love them, but that we are there to guide and protect them along life's journey.

Chapter 8

For Parents Only

Life is what happens to you while you're busy making other plans.

John Lennon

I've saved you for last. Not because parents are less important but because I want you to remember just how vital you are in your child's world. It's so easy for parents to deny themselves rest, private time, and fun because they are more concerned with the good of their children. But the truth is that parents who are happy, fulfilled, and in balance often raise healthier children. Your good health transcends down to your children.

When Was The Last Time You . . .

- Thought about making time for your relationship?
- Felt connected to the outside world?
- Did something for your own personal growth?

Making Time For Yourself

Making time for yourself rejuvenates not only you but your children and your marriage. To do this requires you to acknowledge that as a human being, you count. Consider this for a moment: when you consider a job or career change, don't you think about the vacation and time-off benefits before making a decision? Would you really take a new job that affords you no personal time off? No, because you know that to be effective in your position, you will need time off throughout the year. While parenting is the most important job we will ever know, having some free time to ourselves is key if we are to be effective.

Making time for yourself and adding some diversity to your life is beneficial for these reasons:

✚ Increases self-esteem
✚ Increases overall life satisfaction
✚ Gives your life greater purpose and meaning
✚ Allows you to find your patience and keep it
✚ Improves your ability to be caring and effectual with your kids

Sadly, a lot of people deny themselves this essential element. They put themselves on the back burner because they've been schooled to believe that it's the right thing to do. But when mothers and fathers have interests outside the home or job, they have more realistic expectations of other members of the family. So why do so many parents deny themselves something which would ultimately be beneficial to their children?

✚ Guilt is the biggest diversion
✚ Lack of planning and organization
✚ Complicated, over-committed life styles
✚ Procrastination

So then, how do you change and make time for yourself? First of all, it requires a conscious decision to change and a commitment to start. It also takes the realization and belief that when you take good care of yourself, you are a better parent, partner, and friend. Make it a point to:

+ Toss out that guilt you've been lugging around.
+ Seek out people who have interests similar to yours.
+ Write out as complete a wish list as you can. Include such areas as health and fitness, relationships, dreams, personal growth, spiritual growth, travel, and all the things you would do if you only had the time.
+ Arrange to put 30 minutes into the end of your day for personal reflection.

Getting Out From Under Stress

So much has been written about stress that by this time we all know it can be a killer. Stress is sneaky because it creeps up behind you and crawls into your world without warning. Most

people don't know they're stressed out until they experience some kind of physical ailment. Unfortunately, many times that physical ailment is a heart attack. Take a good look at yourself and learn to notice the signs that tell you to slow down. As for me, I have two ways of knowing that I'm over-taxing my system: first, I start to sigh out loud; and second, my face starts to look all twisted and out of sorts. My husband shows different signs when under stress. He starts to eat as if raised by wolves and raids the kitchen when everyone else has gone to bed. Still others experience headaches, muscle spasms, or an increase in their blood pressure.

One of the keys to changing your life is first take a good look at it. What kind of lifestyle do you lead? Do you build in time for relaxation and fun? Do you even think it's important?

Realizing that you need to make some healthy changes in one's life is the first step to a more balanced lifestyle. Recognizing that you don't need to be all things to everyone is the next step. Making a conscious decision to take stock of your life and to formulate a reasonable plan for change means you're on your way.

Take A Look At Your Lifestyle

1. Consider How Much Caffeine You Consume Every Day

Caffeine is a stimulant that effects your central nervous system. A little perks you up while too much can make you nervous and jittery. Did you know that it takes 24 hours for one cup of coffee to pass through your body? Your body takes the energy normally meant for running sufficiently to expel the caffeine from your body.

Why be concerned about caffeine? Caffeine can increase the supply of adrenaline in your blood at a time when your body is already trying to do the same thing as a result of stress.

Where's the Caffeine?

	mg of caffeine
Coffee:	
Instant, one cup	104
Percolated, one cup	192
Strong Drip, one cup	240
Tea:	
One cup	48–72
Colas:	
One cup	27–54
Chocolate:	
Hot chocolate, one cup	15

---

2. Do You Get Enough Sleep?

So many of us drag ourselves out of bed in the morning wishing that we could dive back in and pull the covers over our heads. Still there are others who agonize all night long wishing that they could just get to sleep. Sleep is vital to our health because it allows our bodies to reenergize for the next day.

Unlike other parts of the world, our society frowns upon resting during the day. People who sneak in a little snooze or a "power nap" in the afternoon are often considered lazy and unmotivated. But they are actually smart because they are listening to their bodies telling them to take a break and rest. Instead of reaching for that cup of coffee around three o'clock, consider resting quietly for 15 minutes.

3. Can You Use A Good Drink?

Routinely reaching for alcohol when under stress has its drawbacks. When you're under stress, alcohol has a tendency to hit you harder because stress increases your metabolism. Initially you may feel relaxed, but the feeling is often short-lived. After a while, you will feel sleepy, drained, and maybe a little depressed.

Some Smoke In Your Eyez . . .

+ It is estimated that one-third of all cancer deaths are caused by smoking.

+ It is estimated that one-fourth of all heart attacks are caused by smoking.

  + Smoking is a factor in approximately 17% of all deaths annually in the US

4. Are You Still Smoking?

Cigarettes and stress are old friends because smoking seems to be a common response to feeling stressed out. Even people who quit will often return to smoking when under stress. Unfortunately, the effects of smoking on the body are quite real and can have disastrous consequences.

There simply isn't anything positive to say about this habit. To put it lightly, smoking negatively effects every organ in the body. When you add stress to the equation, the damage can be all the more serious. The only way to get out from under the toxicity of smoking is to stop.

5. You Are What You Eat

Don't you hate that saying? I know I do. But guess what? It's true. The average person will consume between 50 and 90 tons of food in a lifetime. Like air, water, and sleep, we must have food to live. Therefore, the quality of food we put in our bodies is a major contributing factor to our overall health. When you're rushing to pick this child up from soccer and the other from tutoring the lure of a fast-food restaurant can be pretty strong. I know it's easy. You're exhausted from a hectic day and cooking is the last thing you feel like doing. But resist you must! Fast food tastes good but it's full of no-good fat

Eating Healthy

Include in your diet:

+ start the day with a good breakfast
+ raw fruits and vegetables
+ fish and poultry
+ low-fat foods
+ complex carbohydrates

Avoid in your diet:

+ salt
+ refined sugar
+ alcohol and caffeine
+ fried and fatty foods

calories that you and your children don't need. Try to decrease the number of times you stop at the drive-through for a quick burger, fries, and a shake. Instead, seek out fresh foods low in fat and sodium like chicken or fish.

Stress Busters

The best way to take control of the stress in your life is to treat yourself well. Now hold on, don't go running off thinking that it's impossible. Everything is possible. Keep in mind that taking time out for a little "self-indulgence" isn't selfish, it's essential to your overall health. In time you will notice that feeling healthy and energized is contagious. When you feel terrific, everyone around you tends to feel better too. The box on page 140 offers some quick ideas to get you started:

Once you reach the realization that taking time out for yourself has its benefits, you might want to consider some other ways to relieve your stress.

Easy Ways To Relieve Your Stress

1. Limit the number of obligations you take on at one time.
2. Be realistic with your schedule and don't cram extra things in.
3. Pick out your clothes for the next day the night before.
4. Leave for work 5 minutes earlier and drive slower.
5. Set aside a little time in your day that belongs only to you.
6. When you get home change your clothes and get into something comfortable.
7. Instead of plopping down in front of the TV, play with your kids or hang out with them in their room.
8. Be protective of your leisure time and try not to give it up for another commitment.
9. Turn the TV off at dinner time and instead play soft music and talk with your family.
10. Let one of your weekend days be for relaxation and not chores and shopping.

Exercise

Take a walk. Play golf. Exercise is one of the best ways to rid the body of the harmful effects of stress. Exercise burns off the adrenaline released into your system and instead releases endorphins. Endorphins help to relieve pain and create a feeling of well-being.

A daily regimen of exercise:

✚ Improves digestion
✚ Increases endurance and energy levels
✚ Burns fat
✚ Lowers cholesterol
✚ Elevates your mood
✚ Reduces anxiety and depression

Meditation

Meditation has been practiced for thousands of years but few of us understand what it is. Meditation is one of the best ways to cool down both a stressed-out mind and body. It is beneficial because it is a way to rid the mind of all outside stimuli. There are many techniques such as yoga, tai chi, or the Benson Relaxation Response. Look in your community for local certified classes.

Whatever form of meditation you choose, you are making an important decision to get healthy. Remember that when your body and mind is relieved of stress and in balance, the rest of you is less likely to come apart.

Reconnect With The Outside World

Do you feel like you've pushed out to sea on an ice floe? Does the world look as if it is carrying on without you? It's so easy to be swept away by obligations to family and work. Day in and day out it's the same routine. Gradually you get so absorbed in your "stuff" that the newspapers start to go unread and build up by the back door.

We all need to belong and to be valued. It gives us a sense of purpose and meaning in our lives. If you've disconnected from the world then there's no time like the present to jump back in. Join an organization, take a night school class, or become active in your community. The possibilities are endless.

A Good Circle Of Friends

We all think that we can handle life's obstacles by ourselves but there's nothing like a good circle of friends to lend support and strength when you need it. It's okay to let others

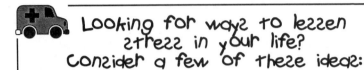

Looking for ways to lessen
stress in your life?
Consider a few of these ideas:

Make time for your relationship:

+ Schedule in a date at least once a month and take in a movie or dinner.
+ Swap your kids with a friend's. You sit for them one night and they'll sit for you another night.

Stay connected to the outside world:

+ Join a volunteer organization in your community.
+ Take a course at a community college or night school program.
+ Enroll in a fitness class like aerobics, karate, cycling, or yoga.

Allow yourself a few indulgences from time to time:

+ Go for a massage, facial, or pedicure.
+ Take those golf lessons.
+ Sleep in late on a Saturday or Sunday.

Take some time out for you during the week:

+ Take a long, hot bubble bath.
+ Rent a favorite video to watch after the kids are asleep.
+ Curl up with a good book or some favorite music.
+ Take a drive along the beach or through the countryside.

help you from time to time. You'll get the opportunity to do the same down the road. I remember as a child my family getting through some difficult moments with the love of good friends.

Resource Guide for Parents Only

Books and Tapes:

• *Chicken Soup for the Soul* (1993). Jack Canfield and Mark Victor Hansen. Deerfield Beach, FL: Health Communications, Inc.

- *Creative Visualization: Use the Power of Your Imagination to Create What You Want in Your Life, Second Edition* (1995). Shakti Gawain. Novato, CA: New World Library.
- *Ageless Mind, Timeless Body* (1993). Deepak Chopra. New York: Random House.
- *The Road Less Traveled* (1978). M. Scott Peck. New York: Simon and Schuster.
- *Fit For Life* (1987). Harvey and Marilyn Diamond. New York: TimeWarner.
- *Life! Reflections On Your Journey* (1995). Louise L. Hay. Carson, CA: Hay House, Inc.
- *The Practical Guide To Practically Everything* (1996). Peter Bernstein and Christopher Ma. New York: Random House.
- *Stress First Aid for the Working Woman: How to Keep Cool When You're Under Fire!* (1991). B.J. Epstein. Carmel, CA: Becoming Press.
- *Prescription For Nutritional Healing, Second Edition* (1997). James F. Balch and Phyllis A. Balch. Garden City, NY: Avery Publishing Group.
- *The Joy of Stress* (1986). Peter G. Hanson. Kansas City, MI: Andrews, McMeel, and Parker.
- *The PDR Family Guide to Women's Health and Prescription Drugs* (1994). Montvale, NJ: Medical Economics.
- *Optimal Wellness* (1995). Ralph Golan. New York: Random House.
- *Total Health for Men* (1995). Edited by Neil Wertheimer. Emmaus, PA: Rodale Press.
- *The Men's Health Book* (1994). Michael Oppenheim. Englewood Cliffs, NJ: Prentice Hall.
- *The 7 Habits of Highly Effective People* (1989). Stephen R. Covey. NewYork: Simon and Schuster.
- *Make the Connection: Ten Steps to a Better Life* (1996). Bob Greene and Oprah Winfrey. New York: Hyperion.
- *How Good Do We Have to Be?* (1996). Harold Kusher. Boston: Little, Brown, and Company.

Resource Guide

Suggested Reading for Parents

Ames, Louise Bates, and Chase Haber, Carol (1989). *He Hit Me First: When Brothers and Sisters Fight.* New York: Warner Books.

Balter, Lawrence, and Shreve, Anita (1989). *Who's in Control? Dr. Balter's Guide to Discipline without Combat.* Las Cruces, CA: Poseidon Press.

Bettelheim, Bruno (1987). *The Good Enough Parent.* New York: Alfred A. Knopf.

Brazelton, T. Berry (1989). *Toddlers and Parents,* rev.ed. New York: Delacorte Press/Lawrence.

Brazelton, T. Berry and Cramer, B. G. (1990). *The Earliest Relationship.* Reading, MA: Addison-Wesley/Lawrence.

Brazelton, T. Berry (1992). *Touchpoints.* Reading, MA: Addison-Wesley/Lawrence.

Clark, Lynn (1989). *The Time Out Solution: A Parent's Guide for Handling Everyday Behavior Problems.* Chicago: Contemporary Books.

DeFrancis, Beth (1994). *The Parent's Resource Guide.* Holbrook, MA: Bob Adams, Inc.

Dinkmeyer, Don, McKay, Gary, and Dinkmeyer, James (1990). *Parenting Young Children.* New York: Random House.

Eisenberg, Arlene, Murkoff, Heidi, and Hathaway, Sandee (1994). *What to Expect: The Toddler Years.* New York: Workman Publishing.

Hardy, Dawn (1992). *Bargains-By-Mail For Baby and You.* Rocklin, CA: Prima Publishing.

Kurcinka, Mary Sheedy (1992). *Raising Your Spirited Child: A Guide for Parents Whose Child is More.* New York: HarperCollins.

Lansky, Vicki (1991). *Getting Your Baby to Sleep . . . And Back to Sleep.* Deephaven, MN: The Book Peddlers.

Lansky, Vicki (1992). *Practical Parenting Tips* rev.ed. Deephaven, MN: Meadowbrook Press.

Leach, Penelope (1989). *Your Baby and Child: From Birth to Age Five.* New York: Alfred A. Knopf.

Oppenheim, Joanne and Oppenheim, Stephanie (1997). *The Best Toys, Books, Videos & Software for Kids 1997.* Rocklin, CA: Prima Publishing.

Philadelphia Child Guidance Center (1993). *Your Child's Emotional Health.* New York: Macmillan.

Pipher, Mary (1996). *The Shelter of Each Other: Rebuilding Our Families.* New York: Grosset/Putnam.

Rosemond, John (1989). *Six-Point Plan for Raising Happy, Healthy Children.* Kansas City, MI: Andrews & McMeel.

Rosemond, John (1993). *Making the Terrible Twos Terrific.* Kansas City, MI: Andrews & McMeel.

Schaefer, Charles, and DiGeronimo, Theresa Foy (1992). *Winning Bedtime Battles: How to Help Your Child Develop Good Sleep Habits.* New York: Carol Publishing.

Sears, William and Sears, Martha (1995). *The Discipline Book.* Boston, MA: Little, Brown and Company.

Spock, Benjamin and Rothenberg, Michael (1992). *Dr. Spock's Baby and Child Care.* New York: Pocket Books.

Stern, Daniel (1977). *The First Relationship.* Cambridge, MA: Harvard University Press.

Taffel, Ron (1991). *Parenting by Heart.* Reading, MA: Addison-Wesley.

Turecki, Stanley (1989). *The Difficult Child*, rev.ed. New York: Bantam Books.

Warren, Paul, and Minirth, Frank (1992). *Things that Go Bump in the Night: How to Help Your Children Overcome Their Natural Fears.* Nashvillle, TN: Thomas Nelson.

Winnicott, D. W. (1988). *Babies and Their Mothers.* Introduction by Benjamin Spock. Reading, MA: Addison-Wesley/ Lawrence.

Suggested Periodicals to Explore

American Baby. Cahners Publishing Co., 475 Park Avenue South, New York, NY, 10016. (212) 689-3600.

Baby Talk. Parenting Unlimited, Inc., 636 Sixth Avenue, New York, NY, 10011. (212) 989-8181.

Child. PO Box 3176, Harlan, IA 51593-0367. (800) 777-0222.

Growing Parent. Dunn and Hargitt, Inc., 22 North Second Street, Lafayette, IN, 47902. (317) 423-2624.

Parenting. Time, Inc., Ventures, 301 Howard Street, 17th Floor, San Francisco, CA, 94105. (800) 635-2665.

Parents Magazine. Gruner and Jahr USA Publishing, 685 Third Avenue, New York, NY, 10017. (212) 878-8700.

Parent's Digest. Meredith Corporation, 1716 Locust Street, Des Moines, IA 50309. (515) 284-3000.

Practical Parenting. King's Reach Tower, Stamford Street, London, SE19LS. 071-261-5058.

Priority Parenting. Tamra B. Orr, P.O. Box 1793, Warsaw, IN, 46581-1793. (219) 268-1415.

Sesame Street Parent's Guide. Children's Television Workshop, One Lincoln Plaza, New York, NY, 10023. (212) 595-3456.

Working Mother. Customer Service Manager, PO Box 5239, Harlan, IA, 51593-0739. (800) 876-9414.

Organizations & Associations

American Academy of Pediatrics
141 Northwest Point Blvd., P.O. Box 927
Elk Grove Village, IL 60009-0927
(800) 433-9016

Association for Childhood Education International (ACEI)
11501 Georgia Avenue, Suite 315
Wheaton, MD 20902
(800) 423-3563

Consumer Product Safety Commission (CPSC)
Office of Information and Public Affairs
5401 West Bard Avenue
Bethesda, MD 20816
(800) 638-CPSC

National Association for the Education of Young Children
    (NAEYC)
1509 16th Street NW
Washington, DC 20036-1826
(800) 424-2460

National Academy of Early Childhood Programs
1834 Connecticut Avenue NW
Washington, DC 20009

National Association for Family Child Care
(800) 359-3817

National PTA
700 North Rush Street
Chicago, IL 60611
(312) 787-0977

Parent Action, The National Association of Parents
2 North Charles Street, Suite 960
Baltimore, MD 21201
(410) 727-3687

Catalogs for Children

Adoption Book Catalog .... (800) 765-2367
Alcazar's Catalog of Childrens' Music .... (800) 541-9904
The American Girls Collection .... (800) 845-0005
Back to Basics Toys .... (800) 356-5360
Childcraft .... (800) 631-5657
Constructive Playthings .... (800) 832-0572
Educational Insights .... (800) 933-3277
Great Kids Company .... (800) 533-2166
Kids First! .... (800) 331-6197
Learning Resources .... (800) 222-3909
Listening Library .... (800) 243-4504
Music for Little People .... (800) 727-2233
National Geographic .... (800) 638-4077
The Nature Company .... (800) 227-1114
One Step Ahead .... (800) 274-8440
Playfair Toys .... (800) 824-7255
Reader's Digest Kids Catalog .... (800) 458-3014
Right Start Catalog.. (800) 548-8531
Sensational Beginnings .... (800) 444-2147
Toys to Grow On .... (800) 874-4242
Videos for Kids .... (800) 521-2832

Helplines

The American Baby Helpline
(900) 860-4888
24 hours a day, 7 days a week
.95¢ per minute

Bright Beginnings Warmline
(412) 641-4546
Monday-Friday, 9 a.m. to 9 p.m. EST

Child Magazine's MediaKids Hotline
(900) 407-4KID
Tuesday-Friday, 9 a.m. to 9 p.m. EST
.95 per call

Parenting Hotline
(900) 535-MOMS
$1.95 for the first minute
.95(for each additional minute

Parents Helpline
(900) 903-KIDS
24 hours a day, seven days a week
.95(per minute

Parents Stressline
(800) 421-0353
Monday-Friday, 8:30 a.m. to 5 p.m., p.s.t.

Suggested Parenting Television Programs

The American Baby	Family Channel
Healthy Kids	Family Channel
Kids These Days	Lifetime Channel
What Every Baby Knows	Lifetime Channel
Your Baby & Child	Lifetime Channel
Your Child Six to Twelve	Lifetime Channel
with Dr. Kyle Pruett	

Suggested Children's Television Programs

Adventures in Wonderland   Disney Channel
Barney & Friends   PBS Channel
Lamb Chop's Play-Along   PBS Channel
Mr. Rogers' Neighborhood   PBS Channel
National Geographic Explorer   TBS Channel
Nick News   Nickelodeon Channel
Reading Rainbow   PBS Channel
Sesame Street   PBS Channel
Where in Time is Carmen Sandiego?   PBS Channel

Children's Radio Programs

Popular Syndicated Shows:

Pickleberry Pie   National Public Radio
Rabbit Ears Radio   Public Radio International

About the Author

Kathy Levinson, Ph.D. grew up on Long Island, New York. As with any family, there are always the normal tribulations mixed with the unusual. Times that make you strong and times that the family still can laugh over. With two rascals as older brothers around, Dr. Levinson learned how to be quick on her feet. When her father died suddenly, she learned about strength and independence from her mom who was faced with the challenge of raising her and her brothers alone. Dr. Levinson realized the special ties only siblings share as she experienced both brothers' service in the military during the Vietnam War. Together, Dr. Levinson and her family learned about perserverence and keeping one's sense of humor in the face of good times and bad.

As a college student, Dr. Levinson earned a bachelor's degree in psychology and elementary education from Hofstra University. She then went on to earn a master's degree and professional diploma in school psychology from Queens College. As a school psychologist, Dr. Levinson worked for several years in the Sewanhaka School District on Long Island.

Feeling the urge to experience other parts of the country, Dr. Levinson moved to Boca Raton, Florida where she met her husband, Marc Levinson, M.D. While working with multiply-disabled students in Palm Beach County Schools, she entered Nova University's doctoral program in family therapy.

After graduating with a Ph.D in family therapy from Nova University, Dr. Levinson went on to open the Mizner Family Institute in Boca Raton.

Dr. Levinson has spoken on a national level on the subject of head injury and is published in her field. She has served as a professional council member of the Florida Association of Head Injury. Currently Dr. Levinson serves on the executive board of Universal Aid for Children, a nonprofit agency that enables families to adopt children from international countries as well as provide medical relief and rescue to disadvantaged children across the world. She is also an active member of the Junior League of Boca Raton.

As a speaker and author, Dr. Levinson enjoys talking to professional and community organizations on the subjects of child development, educational issues, parenting skills, and of course, tantrums. Her first book, *Raising Sensitive Children When the World Seems So Crazy* received acclaim from several sources, including the *Miami Herald.*

Currently, Dr. Levinson is busy not only writing, but developing a successful publishing business. But of all the hats she wears, the most precious is that of mom to her little boy, Peter. Not long ago, Dr. Levinson and her husband were blessed with his arrival from Vietnam on Christmas Eve. Together they share family and home with an enormous English Mastiff named Blue Dog. The Levinson family recently celebrated the arrival of Pete's baby sister, Aimée.

Index